Hattenbeek. 8/6/93
Tywyn

LMS
ENGINE SHEDS

ISBN 1 871608 04 X

FOR MAVIS AND FRIENDS

Published by
IRWELL PRESS
3 Durley Avenue, Pinner, Middlesex, HA5 1JQ
Printed and bound by Netherwood Dalton & Co., Huddersfield

LMS
ENGINE SHEDS

Their History and Development

VOLUME SIX
THE HIGHLAND RAILWAY

Chris Hawkins, George Reeve
& James Stevenson

IRWELL PRESS

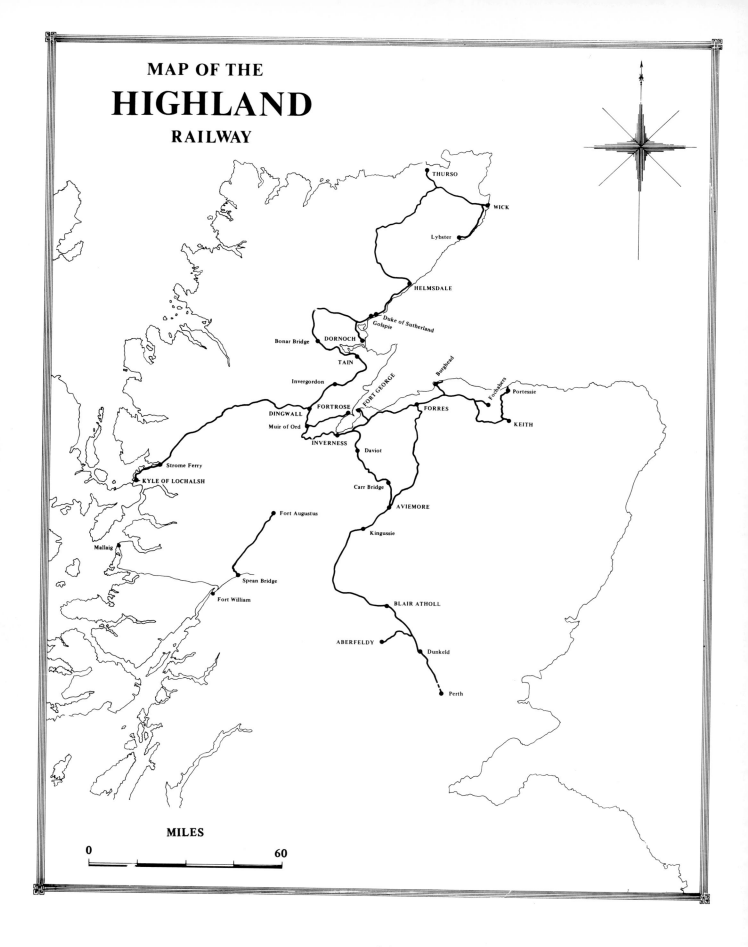

MAP OF THE
HIGHLAND
RAILWAY

THURSO

WICK

Lybster

HELMSDALE

Duke of Sutherland
Golspie

Bonar Bridge

DORNOCH

TAIN

Invergordon

FORT GEORGE

Burghead

Fochabers

Portessie

FORRES

KEITH

DINGWALL

FORTROSE

Muir of Ord

INVERNESS

Daviot

Strome Ferry

KYLE OF LOCHALSH

Carr Bridge

AVIEMORE

Fort Augustus

Kingussie

Mallaig

Spean Bridge

Fort William

BLAIR ATHOLL

ABERFELDY

Dunkeld

Perth

MILES

0   60

CONTENTS

AUTHORS' NOTE

It was previously intended to complete the series *LMS Engine Sheds* with volume six, describing both the Highland and Glasgow and South Western Railway sheds. A fortunate abundance of material and a change of publisher now enables these companies to be dealt with separately so that the final volume will now be No. 7, the G&SWR. It will also contain the 1945 Allocations, omitted so far from the Scottish volumes in this series. The Northern Division, as recounted in Volume 5 ('Authors Note') was perceived very much as 'an entity' beyond that afforded the English Divisions and transfers to and from the south were relatively few. The complete 1945 allocation for Scotland will thus be listed in Volume 7, together with some supplementary allocation details.

To show the comparitive sizes of each location all the track plans have been reproduced at the uniform scale of approximately two chains to one inch.

The first shed at Helmsdale, the railway still something of a scar on the landscape. Its construction reveals it to have been the most primitive shed (for its size) so far unearthed on the Highland and whether it sustained gale damage early on, or the shoring was in anticipation thereof, is not known. *Reproduced with permission from the George Washington Wilson Collection in Aberdeen University Library, Ref. F4254.*

THE
HIGHLAND RAILWAY

If you had travelled over it from end to end you would never again speak of it as a small line

COMPLETION of the unpromising branch from Wick to Lybster (a line worked by the HR but nominally independent) in the Summer of 1903 brought the Highland Railway to its final form, a prosaic end to perhaps the most extraordinary railway construction in Britain. A main line largely of single track, the Highland weaved a course through mountain and moor from the highest passes to the sea.

The genesis of the company lay in November 1855 when the Inverness and Nairn Railway opened fifteen miles of route between these towns, with a small engine shed at Inverness within the area later to be occupied by Lochgorm Works. The line was quickly pushed further east, now by the Inverness and Aberdeen Junction Railway, until Keith, more than fifty miles from Inverness, was reached in August 1858. An end-on junction was formed there with the Great North of Scotland Railway, connecting Inverness with the emerging railway network of the country. The Inverness and Aberdeen Junction provided their own shed at Keith and a four-road building eventually took shape. Much too grand for its purpose half of it was transplanted to Blair Atholl in 1868.

The new route to the south from Inverness was very circuitous and relations with the Great North of Scotland were for many years unhappy. The enmity which came down the years between the Highland and the Great North of Scotland exceeded possibly even that of the Caledonian and North British, and many famous English rivalries, though it did not prevent subsequent amalgamation attempts - an Act of 1899 allowed for the formation of a 'Highland and North of Scotland Railway' by 1907. Thomas Addy Wilson, the General Manager, described meetings between Directors of the two companies as 'frequently of a stormy kind'. It ended, Wilson notes, on January 5th 1860 at a meeting 'more unpleasant than usual' with 'the Aberdeen people' summarily ejected : 'Matheson, the chairman, is reported to have produced his cheque book and said *There is your £40,000 and there is the door*'.

Efforts in the 1840s to build a direct line to the south had failed but in 1861 the Inverness and Perth Junction Railway was formed to build a line over the 105 miles from Forres to Dunkeld which since 1856 had been connected with Perth by a 15 mile branch line, a small shed existing at Dunkeld during the years when it was a terminus. In September 1863 the through route from Forres to Dunkeld and thence to Perth was opened, construction taking no more than two years, a remarkable feat in the circumstances. At the same time a shed was built at Blair Atholl which not only provided banking engines for the climb to Druimuachdar but also bridged the gap between Perth and Forres (where sheds were also provided).

From Inverness construction northwards proceeded only slowly, initially under the aegis of the Inverness and Ross-shire Railway, formed in 1860. Dingwall was secured by 1862 and a small engine was later put up there. Tain had a railway by 1864 and also acquired a shed but it was 1871 before the line reached Helmsdale where the most important of the intermediate sheds was located.

The Highland Railway itself had come into existence in 1865 through the amalgamation of the Inverness and Aberdeen Junction and the Inverness and Perth Junction Railways. Wick was reached in 1874 and Thurso by a branch from Georgemas with engine shed at each terminus. Earlier the Dingwall and Skye Railway had been taken as far as Strome Ferry, where a shed was inevitably provided. Built by separate companies the Wick and Skye lines were worked by the Highland from the start.

The Highland differed markedly from all other major pre-Grouping companies - unlike any other it served a distinct community, isolated and scattered. It had been forged by local people against odds that were sometimes staggering, local gentry who remained in control of the company's destiny. It faced an almost constant financial peril which forced it to ever greater efforts of economy and improvisation. The editor of *The Railway Magazine* pursued this line of enquiry with Thomas Addy Wilson, the General Manager, in 1899 :

'Where did all the money come from for these various costly works, may I ask, for I understood you to say at the outset that the Highland Railway was a Highland creation and due to local enterprise?'

'That is a question which it is a delight to answer, because it brings out a self-sacrificing feature in Highland character where the absolute good of the country is concerned, which is comparatively rare in the commercial history of modern times. The financial situation was summed up some years ago by Mr. Dougall, a former manager, in these sentences : *On the completion of the various lines it was found that, although the proprietors and others in the district had subscribed largely towards them, £1,200,000 was required to equip and open them for traffic. This money had to be raised, and the directors gave their personal security to the banks and insurance offices, the whole of them becoming thus, jointly and severally, responsible for the amount. The obligation continued for ten years, but in consequence of the steady development of the traffic, it was ultimately discharged without the directors losing a single sixpence.'* The turn of the century eulogising tendencies of *The Railway Magazine* apart, the Highland was the most distinctly 'local' of the LMS constituents, a fierce independence enhanced by physical isolation.

A particular feature of the Highland was the branch lines which it operated (but which it did not in all cases build). Burghead (1862), Aberfeldy (1865), Portessie (1884), Fochabers (1893), Fortrose (1894), Fort George (1894), Dornoch (1902) and Lybster (1903), each as a terminus acquired engine sheds although that at Portessie lasted only until 1907. Even shorter-lived was the tiny shed at Kinloss opened by the Findhorn Railway in 1860, taken over by the Inverness and Aberdeen Junction in 1862 and closed with the branch in 1869.

The end of the nineteenth century saw also the extension of the Dingwall and Skye Railway forward from Strome Ferry to Kyle of Lochalsh. This was opened in 1897 and a handsome stone shed at Kyle replaced the rickety wooden structure at the former terminus. Between 1903 and 1907 the Highland worked the Invergarry and Fort Augustus Railway, from its junction with the West Highland Railway at Spean Bridge. Sheds were provided both at Spean Bridge and at Fort Augustus but only the latter was ever used.

At its peak the Highland operated over 500 route miles. Its main line covered 272 miles between Wick and Stanley Junction, whence running powers were exercised over the Caledonian to Perth. Indeed before the opening of the Direct line the corresponding mileage was 293¾ almost identical to that between London and Carlisle. Its building is a story of fortitude in the face of daunting engineering difficulties and unpromising financial prospects, but throughout its life the railway benefitted greatly (as we have seen) from the generosity of many Highland Landowners, particularly the Duke of Sutherland who contributed vastly to the construction of the North line, financing on his own the Brora to Helmsdale section. From 1870 until nationalisation the Third Duke and his successors possessed their own engine and two coaches which they were permitted to use on the North line, a 'ducal engine shed' standing first at Brora but later at Golspie. This is perhaps the oddest of all the 'LMS Sheds' to be described in this series.

Money, or rather the want of it, haunted the

Belladrum **at Inverness, certainly the most extravagant of the Highland sheds and possibly the most grandiose in Scotland. It occupied a damp, mournful site;** from *The Locomotive : Early locomotives of the Inverness and Nairn and Inverness and Aberdeen Junction Railways were delivered by sea from Leith to Inverness where they were unloaded at the Canal Basin and brought to Lochgorm, so called from a small pond or lakelet which formerly occupied the site of the present running shed.* Photo:- Authors Collection.

The small wooden engine shed was to be found dotted about the Highland, and varied little in its nature over many years. Lybster was more or less the last, excluding replacements, and scarcely differed from its predecessors of half a century or so before. *Photo:- F.Moore*

Perth around 1903. This was the second of the only two large sheds to be found on the Highland; it entirely contrasted with the Inverness roundhouse and though it reflected a Highland (more exactly, a Scottish) taste for the massive it was conventional in its straight layout, including primitive 'coal bench'. *Photo:- Brian Hilton Collection*

Highland from its earliest days; Wilson lamented this and longed for some of the problems which beset his contemporaries further south. The 'colossal and varied industries . . . . . . with their teeming populations' which presented such difficulties elsewhere were entirely absent in the Highlands of Scotland and the General Manager dreamed of. . . . .'just half a score of really big towns'.

Ever impecunious, expenditure which might be routine on other lines was 'sheer extravagance' on the HR. There was, Wilson said, a great deal 'of what we term unremunerative traffic' and though the engine sheds were hardly lavish most, when they were not burning down or falling prey to tempest, were at least solidly built.

Notice

The special attention of Firemen, Drivers and Washers Out and all concerned is being drawn to the fact that nearly all the Locomotive Boilers on this railway are becoming choked up with dirt both waterspaces of tubes and fireboxes in consequence of which the consumption of coal is being considerably increased besides the metal of tubes being greatly wasted. To remedy this I have to request that immediate steps be taken to have all boilers properly and regularly washed out and hope I shall not have to complain of this in future.

Signed D. Jones, Loco Engineer, 19th July 1894

Latest in a constant stream of missives, Jones' *Notice** to the sheds draws attention to the primitive nature of the engine servicing arrangements on the Highland. Apart from mechanical plant provided by the LMS at Inverness in the 1930s these never really changed much, nor did they have to. There were never the sheer numbers of engines which drove the English companies to ever more elaborate and intensive coaling measures and the simple 'coal bench' staffed by often a single coalman sufficed for Highland needs. The shed buildings themselves were frequently grand in their execution but were often somehow mismatched, perhaps through a tendency to run out of cash as a project advanced. Thus the ornate Marble Arch at Inverness stood remote from the roundhouse it served and in stark contrast

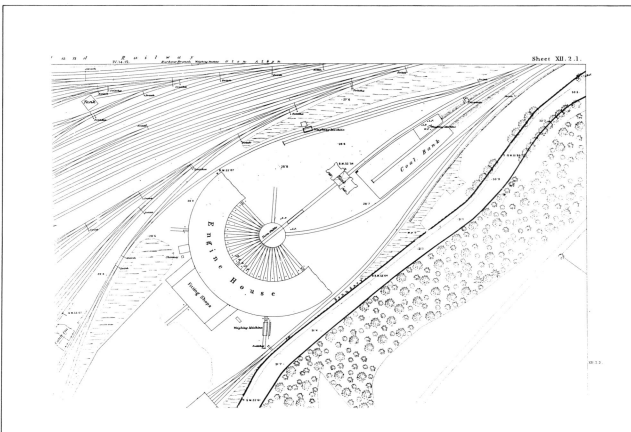

The Inverness roundhouse more or less as built, in the late 1860s, in the 'splendid isolation' which remained such an abiding quality. The 'Marble Arch' even in plan form is clearly a substantial structure and a contrast to the coaling bench, a simple raised area much like an afterthought. The internal sweep of the roundhouse is perhaps the most familiar Highland feature of all, much photographed and instantly recognisable. Unheard of, so far at least, is any view of the 'outside' of the building, an extraordinary curving wall facing a quiet, probably more or less deserted yard, and a complete contrast to the clamour only feet away inside the roundhouse.

to the nearby coal bench, little more (at first) than an area of raised ground. Keith was too big and half of it (see earlier) was subsequently pinched for use elsewhere ; obscure sheds, massively built in stone, seemed to lurk about the Highlands, long disused as the line was pushed further onward.

There was little machinery to accompany any of the Highland engine sheds and Inverness and the Lochgorm Works lay conveniently at the centre of the radiating HR system. A line through the rear of the roundhouse provided for a set of shear legs but little else seems to have been provided. With such long distances it seems inconceivable that simple lifting gear was not also available at Wick, Perth and Kyle.

Turntables by the 1870s were a little over 40ft in diameter with the largest at the most important locations increased to 45ft or thereabouts. 50ft or 55ft was common by the turn of the century and apart from the Inverness example, 55ft sufficed for most uses until the end of steam.

*He was fond of this and firmly in the 'iron mould' of the Chief Engineers, characteristics particularly marked in the Scottish strain and passing with legend into the south of England. Some days before his orders regarding washing out he had fined an apprentice, Jas MacKenzie, 2/6d (12.5p) 'for smoking on the premises during working hours'.

TURNTABLES IN 1920

Wick	55' 0"
Thurso	51' 11"
Lyster	46' 3"
Georgemas	46' 3"
Helmsdale	55' 0"
Golspie	21' 0"
Lairg	50' 0"
Tain	50' 0"
Dingwall	43' 6"
Kyle of Lochalsh	50' 0"
Muir of Ord	50' 0"
Fortrose	50' 0"
Inverness	63' 4"
Forres	48' 6"
Keith	50' 4"
Portessie	45' 0"
Grantown	48' 0"
Aviemore	55' 0"
Kingussie	50' 0"
Blair Atholl	55' 3"
Perth	54' 9"

Ben Rinnes on the Inverness turntable, as LMS No. 14405. Highland turntables, particularly in the earlier years, ran to an assortment of sizes; most other companies were content to list 'tables to standard lengths, 46ft., 50ft., 55ft. or whatever but the Highland was more precise. This was probably a reflection of its chronic shortage of cash, with turntables generally no larger then was absolutely necessary. The Inverness 'table began more modestly (see page 2) but as enlargements were needed considerations of fixed track geometry demanded that it be longer 'then was strictly necessary for the traffic.' *Photo:- T.Middlemass*

Aberfeldy on 13th June 1936 0-4-4Ts of Caledonian origin characterised the line for many years, from about 1930, replacing a variety of Highland tank and tender classes. *Photo: W.A.Camwell*

Aberfeldy

The Perth - Forres main line began operating in 1863 and shortly after, in July 1865, a branch of 8¾ miles was opened from Ballinluig Junction, some 23 miles or more north of Perth to Aberfeldy running west up the valley of the Tay. There were no tank engines available; the line must needs have been at first worked by tender engines, 2-2-2 or more probably a 2-4-0. Money for new construction was in the shortest possible supply and it was therefore decided to rebuild No. 12 *Belladrum*, a 2-4-0 with 6 ft. coupled wheels, to a 2-2-2T; the engine was completed in 1871, possessed of a most unfortunate appearance.

A shed was built at Aberfeldy for the opening of the branch, a primitive wooden affair in keeping with its early occupant; it burnt down in 1902 and a more substantial replacement put up, again in wood. Initially no turntable was provided but in the 1880s one of 26ft. was installed, also one at Ballinluig, allowing the branch engine provided it was a small tank, always to run chimney first. The Ballinluig 'table was taken out in 1916 and the Aberfeldy one about the same time, certainly by 1920. Coaling was effected from a small wagon parked alongside. The long loading bank running parallel with the shed seems to have been used in conjunction with the near-by stone crushing plant or something of that sort. Whatever, the track had been lifted by 1950. Latterly the shed was in a poor state of   repair, part of the roof missing and for a time requiring shoring beams on one of the walls.

Old No. 12 acquired the name *Breadalbane* on arrival at the shed and struggled on until 1879, when it was replaced by No. 17, one of the Jones 2-4-0Ts intended for shunting but pressed into service as branch engines, converted to 4-4-0Ts between 1885 and 1887. No. 17 assumed the name *Breadalbane* on arrival altered to *Aberfeldy* in 1886.

In 1906 the engine, renumbered 50 in 1900, was replaced at Aberfeldy by Yankee Tank No. 102 which was still here in 1919, although it had a spell on the Black Isle branch after 1910. The Highland had intended to build a ninth 0-6-4T for Aberfeldy but in the end this did not materialise. Occasionally, however, one of these worked the branch e.g. No.39 in 1913, as did one or two of the Perth 4-4-0s, No.14382 *Loch Moy* and 14387 *Loch Gerry* in LMS days. Eventually CR 0-4-4Ts became the regular power, until 1960, although 2F 0-6-0 No. 17415 was there in August 1939.

BR 2-6-4T No. 80093 was the branch engine on 23rd September 1961 but it is believed that diesel traction took over soon afterwards; in the last years a Type 2 could be seen rattling up and down on the single brake composite which usually sufficed and on certain runs was marshalled into a mixed train. The shed may have seen some use after this for it was still standing and rail-connected when the last train ran on 1st May 1965, two coaches hauled by D5335.

The dark outlines of Craig Odhar, Tairneachan and Creag Loisgte make for an imposing backdrop when the station is seen from the east. The minute shed is on the extreme left of the photograph. *Photo:- Reproduced with permission from the George Washington Collection in Aberdeen University Library, Ref. D2055*

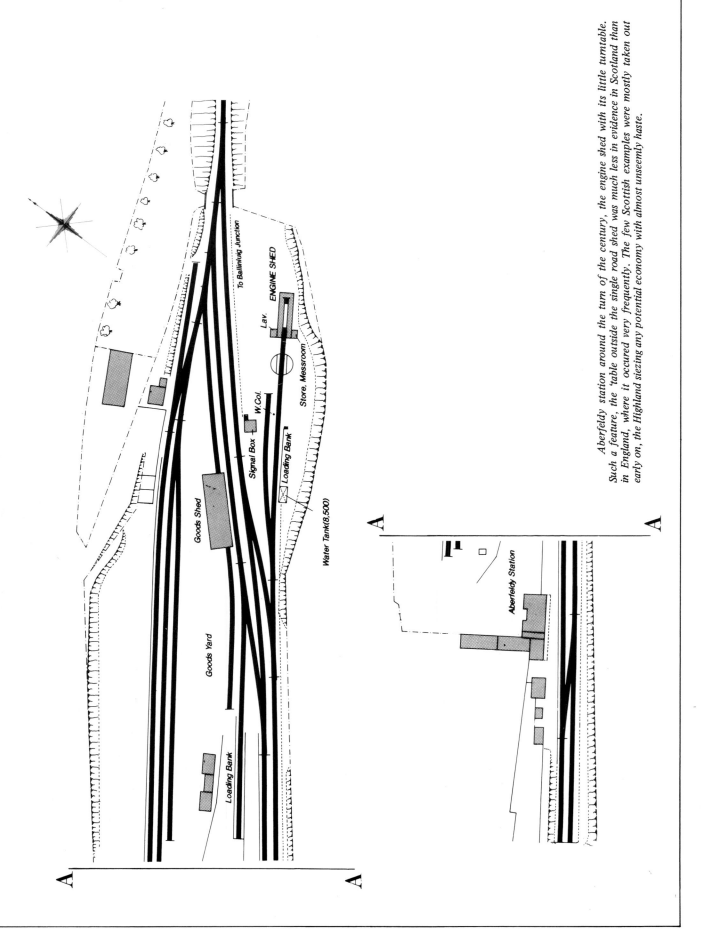

Aberfeldy station around the turn of the century, the engine shed with its little turntable. Such a feature, the 'table outside the single road shed was much less in evidence in Scotland than in England, where it occured very frequently. The few Scottish examples were mostly taken out early on, the Highland siezing any potential economy with almost unseemly haste.

Goods Yard

Goods Shed

Loading Bank

Loading Bank

Signal Box

W.Col.

Water Tank(8,500)

To Ballinluig Junction

Lav.

ENGINE SHED

Store. Messroom

Aberfeldy Station

A

A

A

A

June 1936. 'The branch engine shed' was a minor British, as well as a Highland, institution, though it was disposed irregularly about the country. It thrived, in the main, paradoxically, on the less prosperous concerns, on the Great Eastern and Highland in particular but also on the Great Western. This was in marked contrast to companies like the Midland and LNWR and a minor puzzle of the science of economics.   *Photo:- W.A.Camwell*

The Aberfeldy stone crushing plant, an obscure concern which seems to have failed, certainly by about 1950, and possibly some years prior to that.   *Photo:- A.B.MacLeod*

20th September 1952. By this time the shed was in sorry state, doomed like many Highland sheds to a tumbledown dereliction. Aberfeldy's was a typical story, the first building burning to ash, the second slowly decaying. *Photo:-J.L.Stevenson*

No. 55209 on Wednesday, 24th June 1953. *Photo:- R.F.Roberts*

Aberfeldy on 29th July 1958. The British country terminus seemed mostly to be just that; it reached only to the edge of town, for reasons of expense and the compromise of opposing and promoting interests and thereafter frequently remained surrounded by fields and relatively open country. Aberfeldy despite the surrounding fields was closer to the town than most and homes now stand on the site. *Photo:- Brian Hilton*

Frequently deserted, the Aberfeldy terminus nevertheless came alive upon the branch trains' arrival, a local institution and regarded accordingly until the general decline of the 1960s. The 0-4-4T would leave Ballinluig with mixed train - a coach, wagons *and brake van*, the bunker piled high as if a journey of eighty miles were in prospect, rather than one of eight (it made sense of course, but the sight was nevertheless startling). This merry procession was rendered even more peculiar on dieselisation, a Type 2, then such a very modern machine, rattling up and down, incongrously, with a single coach on the branch service. *Photo:- Lens of Sutton*

Aviemore on 27th September 1935, stone built and distinguished as possibly the largest engine shed, in its original condition (more or less) operated by a preservation concern. The Strathspey Railway presumably inherited the Highland water supply, a small loch feeding a 16,300 gallon water tank.   *Photo:- W.A. Camwell*

Aviemore

Nestling in spectacular mountain country of great beauty, between the Cairngorms and the Monadh Liath, Aviemore became an important junction on the Highland main line, when the Direct Line to Inverness opened in 1898, taking its leave of the old route *via* Forres. The new line, through Carr Bridge and Daviot, was made in three stages in the six years from 1892 and the shed was ready for use upon its completion, in 1898. A much earlier shed also may have existed, for a description of the opening of the original line Dunkeld to Forres through Aviemore in 1863 relates . . . . .'Engine Houses are to be found at Blair Athole, [later altered to Blair-Atholl] Kingussie *and Aviemore'*. A plan of 1871 however does not reveal any building obviously arranged as an engine shed and nothing further is known of this early 'Engine House', whether it derived from the working of the line in sections as it was built, or what caused its (presumably premature) demise. Once it found itself a junction, with passenger trains from the south dividing and those from the north combined, as well as the frequent rearrangement of goods wagons,

Aviemore certainly required a substantial engine shed. Passenger trains would arrive within a few minutes of each other, one from Inverness and one from the Forres line, each conveying portions for Edinburgh and for Glasgow, marshalled accordingly. In some cases a dining car might be attached. There was corresponding marshalling work, additions etc, in the down direction. Freight shunting was also heavy at times and assisting engines were maintained for all three routes centred on the junction, but mainly for the climb to the Slochd. Over the years the Aviemore allocation remained fairly steady at around a dozen, a variety of classes, mainly 4-4-0s in Highland days but strengthened with some Castles in the 1930s and in 1936-7 with a Jones Big Goods. It was also the latter-day home for the two large Cumming 4-4-0s built for the North line, *Durn* and *Snaigow*, as well as for three Big Bens, No. 14417, which was at Aviemore over ten years and Nos. 14418 and 14419, which had much briefer stays. After the war, in 1946, two Clans arrived and stayed until withdrawn in 1947/8, Nos. 14762 *Clan Campbell* and 14764 *Clan Munro*.

(From left to right) 14398 *Ben Alder*, 14379 *Loch Insh* and 14690 *Dalcross Castle* at Aviemore on 9th April 1946. Much of the Highland system lay exhausted by the end of the Second World War for as in the Great War, traffic levels had leapt, redoubling and taxing the long and lonely main line to its limits. In the long summer of 1946 the Highland sheds could begin again the unhurried stabling of engines, with mountains in benign mood. *Photo:- H.C.Casserley*

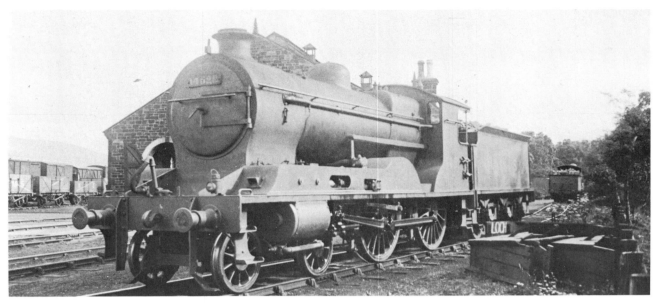

14522 *Snaigow*, probably in the early - mid 1930s.   *Photo:- M.D.England*

In August 1937 the complement was made up entirely of Highland engines, 4-4-0s Nos. 14379 *Loch Insh* and 14381 *Loch Ericht*; 4-6-0s Nos. 14677 *Dunrobin Castle*, 14682 *Beaufort Castle*, 14685 *Dunvegan Castle* and 14692 *Darnaway Castle*; Barney 0-6-0 No. 17696 and Big Goods 4-6-0 No. 17920. There were two passenger turns to Inverness over the Forres line and two via Carr Bridge, a stopping freight to Forres and back, a couple of treble-shifted main line pilots and a station pilot which had a busy time of it. In addition there were regular ballast trains and periodical livestock workings in connection with sales at Kingussie and Grantown. Assistance to Slochd was required for almost all freights and the heavier passenger trains, notably the down sleeping car workings.

In 1939 the work of station pilot, hitherto normally a 4-4-0, was taken over by Caledonian 0-4-4Ts, No. 15213 at first, replaced in succession by 15133, 15174 and finally 55173, prior to dieselisation. Caledonian 4-4-0s also began to appear in the early war years but in 1942 the allocation was still predominantly Highland:

'Aviemore M.P.D. 19th October 1942:
HR 3P Castle 4-6-0 : 14682 *Beaufort Castle*, *14690 Dalcross Castle*, 14692 *Darnaway Castle*.
CR 3P Superheated Dunalastair III 4-4-0: 14434
CR 2P Dunalastair II 4-4-0 : 14338
HR 2P Ben 4-4-0 : 14398 *Ben Alder*, 14399 *Ben Wyvis*
HR 2P Loch 4-4-0 : 14379 *Loch Insh*
CR 2P 0-4-4T : 15133
HR 3F Barney 0-6-0 : 17699, 17700
G & SW R 4F 2-6-0 : 17826
Total 12. Equivalent Booked Engine Turns - 9'.

About this time LMS 2-8-0s first appeared; working from Grangemouth shed they hauled considerable loads of timber south from extensive sidings laid in at the north end of Aviemore. The engines came north with empties and the Grangemouth men lodged at Aviemore. Class 5 4-6-0s had been regular visitors to the shed since the first; No. 5023 worked north from Perth in August 1934 and for a time from 1944 two were based at Aviemore, 5136 and 5138.

By 1950 Caledonian engines had supplanted all the old Highland classes, 3P 4-4-0s Nos. 54455, 54466, 54488 and 54493, 3F 0-6-0 No. 57586 and 0-4-4T No. 55174, accompanying a 5MT 4-6-0, No. 45018. By this time the Great North of Scotland shed at Boat of Garten had been made 'sub' to Aviemore, although engines were still provided from Keith GNS. Freight services on the Speyside line were extended through to Aviemore, bringing GNS 4-4-0s at first and later such oddities as a J36 0-6-0 and a K2 mogul. When the railbuses came to Scotland in the late 1950s the Speyside passenger service ran to and from Aviemore and Boat of Garten shed was closed. (A railbus was also used on a daily stopping service to Inverness and back).

Aviemore appears to have gone out of use in mid-1966, 'for operating purposes' though since dieselisation had come fully to the Highlands, in 1960-61, it had been partially abandoned. It had been dependent upon a high level of traffic worked in traditional fashion and even in 1957 staff had numbered about 130, 70 of them on the locomotive side. By 1961 a single diesel shunter was based there, D2410 at first but later D3896. Aviemore had been coded 29J under Perth in 1935 and 32B, as part of the new Inverness District, in 1940. Its BR code from 1949 was 60B. The shed served for some years as the yard for the local motor dealer but is now restored to its original purposes, in the care of the Strathspey Railway.

14

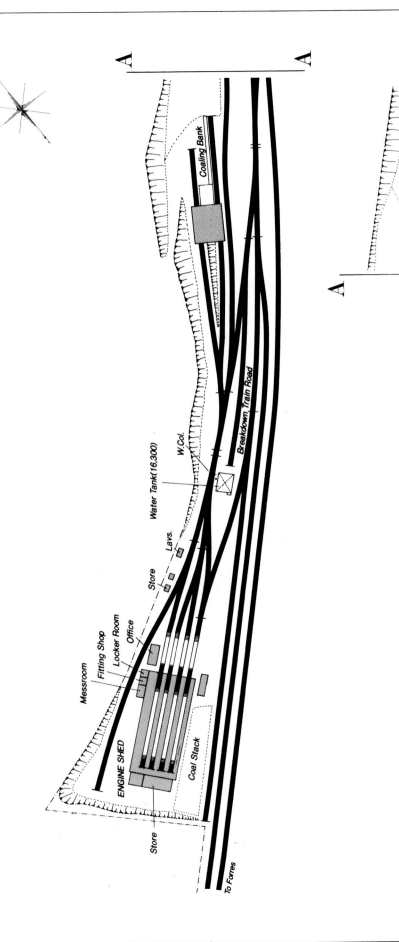

Aviemore in Highland days, now perfectly suited home to the Strathspey Railway. A sort of international 'Ski and mountain centre' it today has a cosmopolitain quality undreamed of in its long years of remoteness, when the station was the focus of contact with a world beyond the mountains.

14379 *Loch Insh,* an engine regularly to be found at Aviemore. The two World Wars did indeed prove enormous peaks in the working of the Highland but The Great Slump from 1929 and a rundown in the Navy (there was little of the tourist interest which reaches every corner of the Scottish Mountains today) made for less traffic. Even so the shed kept an allocation of eight - ten engines, though latterly two or three turns were taken over by class 5s on cyclic workings.

Photo:- H.C.Casserley

Aviemore in August 1936. The class 5 4-6-0s had turned up at the shed regularly since their introduction two years before; two were actually allocated for a while from 1944 (see text) and increasingly through the 1950s it was usual to see one or more at the shed.   *Photo:- A.N.H.Glover*

Off an Inverness freight, Big Goods No. 17926 stands on the old Aviemore 'table, before a splendid HR signal gantry. The turntable had long been 55ft., adequate for any Highland needs as well as the new Stanier 4-6-0s but advancing years and increasing wartime use brought operational problems. Replacement was first agreed in 1943 under the continuing 'Turntable Renewal Programme' but a 'proposed new 60ft. diameter turntable' was still under discussion on 29th October 1947, when the age of the exisiting 55ft. 'table was noted as 50 years. The new turntable appears to have been finally installed in 1948/49.   *Photo:- J.L.Stevenson*

Aviemore in September 1959. Visits throughout the 1950s found engines, class 5s with perhaps a Caledonian 4-4-0, often apparently unattended - 'always in the yard during daytime.'   *Photo:- Photomatic*

The variety of locomotives to be found at Aviemore, after its mountain location, was the most endearing (and enduring) quality of the shed. Its thirteen engines of 1919 had included a Castle, five Small Bens, five Lochs, one Lochgorm Bogie, No. 72A and the 2-4-0 No. 35A, which clung on until 1923. By 1930 the two Cumming 4-4-0s *Snaigow* (see page 14) and *Durn* were present followed by two or three Big Bens. After the Second World War 4-6-0s, 14764 *Clan Munro* and 14767 *Clan MacKinnon* were at the shed, spending their last days, with *Loch Insh, Ben Alder* and Caledonian 4-4-0s, 14363 (Dunalastair IV) 14434 (Dunalastair III Superheated) and 14493 (Pickersgill). There were 3F 0-6-0s, 17597 and 17634, and an 0-4-4T, No. 15133, which had arrived by 1945.   *Photo:- A.B.MacLoed*

Ex - CR 4-4-0 No. 54466 on 8th September 1953. The Aviemore coal 'bench' was actually rather more substantial then many to be found in Scotland and survived long, despite a flimsy construction. It is thought to have been re-clad and improved at some late time.   *Photo:- Tony Wright*

54466 again, inside the shed, on 26th. July 1953. Some work had been done to the roof since Highland days, possibly at the same time as attention had been given to the coal stage. A network of (second hand, most likely) steel framing and supports went up and corrugated cladding applied. The height of the central vent was reduced and the smoke 'pots' (see opposite) disappeared, replaced by longitudinal 'slit' venting. *Photo:- Brian Morrison*

Coaling at Aviemore in time-honoured fashion. Diesels and railbuses continued to stable in the yard whilst Aviemore remained a junction, and the shed languished; it seems finally to have been given up towards the middle part of 1966.

Photo:- Brian Hilton

Blair Atholl shed, transplanted from Keith block by block and rebuilt, with the superlatives of economy that characterised the Highland. 'What would, on lines blessed with a greater populace and the varied traffics to match it, be regarded as worthy of disposal, on our line must wherever it proves possible, be put to some further good'.   *Photo:- H.C.Casserley collection*

Blair Atholl

Blair Atholl lies on the Highland main line and was principal intermediate operating centre of the long stretch between Perth and Aviemore. The eighteen mile climb to Druimuachdar Summit begins here and banking was necessary from the first. To house the engines a wooden shed, 100 ft. by 18 ft. with a 20 ft. turntable immediately outside opened with the line in 1863. It lay at the Perth end of the station, behind the north bound platform, backing onto the road at that point. This shed enjoyed only a brief existence - perhaps it was burnt or blown down - and the Board in January 1868 resolved that a new shed be built, at the Inverness end of the station, to be ready by the following August. They also directed that 'one half' of the generously-proportioned stone-built shed at Keith 'be demolished . . . . . . and the materials be used' for the new structure. A new turntable was probably provided, and certainly by 1881 a 42 ft. example was in use, extended to 46 ft. 6 ins. between 1887 and 1890. A Minute of 25th October 1898 records a 'New Large Steel Girder Turntable . . . . . . 55 ft. diameter . . . . . . for turning the Heaviest class of Engines at Blair Atholl is nearing completion . . . . . when the necessary extension and slueing of sidings consequent on the laying down of this 'table has been completed the double water column arrangement for watering two Engines of a train at one time at the north end of the station will be carried out'. The Appendix to the Working Timetable of 1901 however records the Blair Atholl 'table still at 46 ft. *8* ins and the 'New Large Steel Girder Turntable' is presumed to have been commandeered for use elsewhere*. Blair Atholl eventually received a larger 'table but it was in its turn second hand, a survey of 1948 recording that it had been built in 1893 by the Rose Foundry, Inverness, and was subsequently enlarged to 55 ft. 3 ins, according to the *Appendix to the Working Timetable* of 1907.

The Working Timetables of the 1880s and later give interesting details of the trains to be assisted, either to Dalnaspidal, returning light, or through to Newtonmore where the engine was to turn and come back on an up train. Until about 1900 2-4-0 goods tender engines would have been used on this work, along with older 4-4-0s of the 60 class. The line was doubled from Blair Atholl

*A 55 ft. turntable was installed at Daviot, of all places, around 1898 and this may conceivably have been the one originally intended for Blair. If so, the reasoning is hard to follow.

'Banking Tank' at Blair Atholl, 15th May 1928, the weightiest engines on the line when built 1909 -1911. Intended for heavy work like the Druimuachdar climb, about half the class of eight were at Blair until withdrawal began in the 1930s. They usually stood in the yard to await the next climb, two or perhaps more in a row, but only one remained by late 1935. *Photo:- H.C.Casserley*

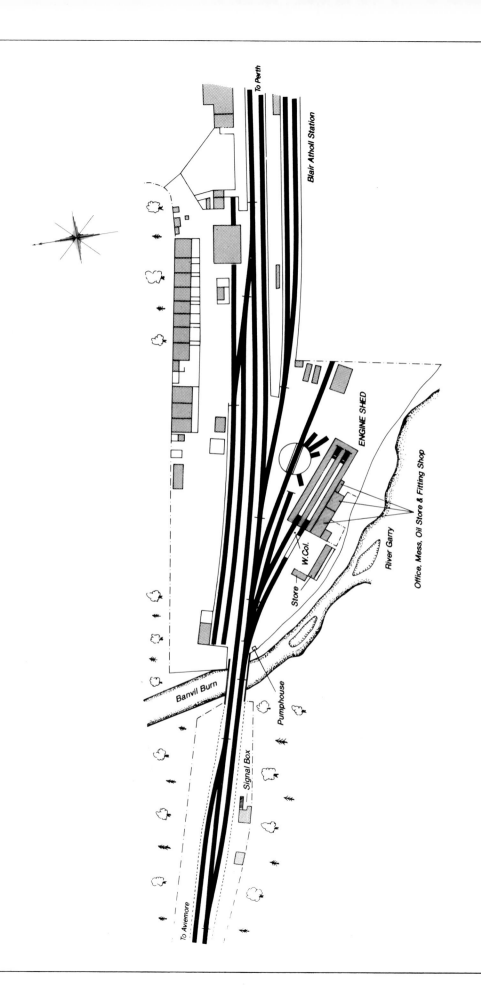

Blair Atholl around the time of the Great War. The shed had a slightly 'out of true' look, deriving no doubt from its block-by-block transfer from Keith, the nicest illustration so far discovered, probably, of the Highlands' chronic impecuniosity. Blair Atholl shared the familar qualities of the 'banking shed', an institution more widespread, by some chance, on the constituents of the LMS than elsewhere. Blair, Beattock, Tebay and Oxenholme, all were crucial to the life of an isolated community, a centre of 'raison d'etre' of a tight-knit settlement.

To Perth

Blair Atholl Station

ENGINE SHED

Store — W.Col.

River Garry

Office, Mess, Oil Store & Fitting Shop

Banvil Burn

Pumphouse

Signal Box

To Aviemore

The Highland tanks did not enjoy a particularly long life and from the early 1930s a variety of bankers, whatever might be available really, was used. Engines coupled in front if the train was to call at Dalnaspidal, such as *Loch Moy* (above) with No. 5025 in July 1935. Briefly around 1937 a pair of G & SWR 0-6-2Ts were in service; one, No. 16902, waits a banking trip on the right, in the traditional 'lye'.   *Photo:- G. E. Langmuir*

The buildings' uneasy transfer from Keith left it with curiously unsatisfactory features. It had a roof much like Aviemore, with strategically sited smoke ventilators, one for each of four carefully positioned locomotives (again, economy) and a central raised vent to take away the remaining smoke. A few blocks were mislaid in the move from Keith, from the appearance of the rear part of the shed and the purpose of the dormer is unclear. It seemed to extend across the width of the shed and may have housed some form of lifting gear (if any was ever provided) and may relate to the rebuilding of the shed. *Photo:- W.A.Camwell*

to Druimuachdar in 1900-1901 to facilitate the growing traffic and the return of banking engines detached at Dalnaspidal. The banking engines and two or three 4-4-0s on local passenger work remained an abiding feature of operations at Blair Atholl. Engines always seem to have been dropped off at Dalnaspidal (unless they were going forward to Newtonmore etc) even while County March Box at the summit was open between 1901 and 1908.

Between 1909 and 1911 Drummond built eight 0-6-4 Banking Tanks primarily for use between Blair Atholl and Dalnaspidal and these must have greatly increased banking efficiency as well as providing the crews with hitherto unimagined comfort on the long descents. Four or five of these engines were usually to be found at Blair Atholl. Instructions varied from time to time on whether engines assisting at the rear were to be coupled to the train or not; Highland practice generally demanded

Jones was moved to provide a 'barracks' in 1894:

Notice

Dormitory at Blair Atholl

This dormitory has been specially fitted up for the benefit of Enginemen and Firemen who may be stationed at Blair Atholl as spare men: and will also be for the use of Enginemen and Firemen arriving at Blair Atholl and having time to rest themselves but not having sufficient time at their disposal to look for lodging elsewhere.

It must be distinctly understood that the Dormitory will be used solely [sic] as a bedroom for the benefit of those requiring it, and as such must be kept as clean as circumstances will permit.

It will be under the charge of the Loco. Foreman and will be locked up when not in use.

Should any damage be done to any portion thereof by any of the occupants during his stay he will be held responsible for cost of repairs.

[signed] D. Jones, Loco Engineer

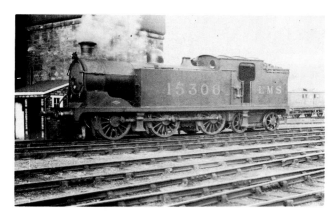

Banking Tank No. 15306. *Photo:- H.N.James*

Ex- Caledonian 4-6-0 No. 14652 outside the shed, probably on a local working from Perth.   *Photo:- C.Brown*

this with respect to goods trains but this was not the case in LMS days. If a passenger train due to call at Dalnaspidal had to be assisted the assisting engine was usually coupled ahead.

The 0-6-4Ts had a fairly short life, the last having gone by the end of 1936, and for a time two G & SW 0-6-2Ts, Nos. 16902 and 16907, were put to use. They were ousted in 1938 by LMS standard 2-6-2Ts, five of which, Nos. 185-189, were allocated new to Perth and spent much of their time at Blair Atholl. Their stay was short and during the war years when banking calls were particularly heavy, most of the work was performed by Caledonian 3P 4-4-0s, of both McIntosh and Pickersgill designs; one or two were still there in late 1959. The

1935; Nos. 14382 *Loch Moy*, 14384 *Loch Laggan*, 14392 *Loch Naver*, 14397 *Ben-y-Gloe* and 14410 *Ben Dearg* and banking engines Nos. 15306, a Drummond ex-HR 0-6-4T and 16902, a Drummond ex-GSWR 0-6-2T.

The Highland engines had been either withdrawn or transferred north by 1940 and local services were worked by Caledonian 4-4-0s, or whatever else Perth could turn out, including LMS 4F 0-6-0s, the occasional Standard Compound and even a North British Glen. These services were taken over by DMUs by 1959 and finally withdrawn in May 1965.

By June 1959 engines at the shed comprised only a pair of 2-6-4Ts, Nos. 42169 and 80126, and

Loch No. 14384 *Loch Laggan* on 15th May 1928. Until this time and for a few years or more HR engines maintained a hegemony. In addition to five 0-6-4 Banking Tanks in 1919 there had been a Small Ben, No. 14 *Ben Dearg* and five Straths, Nos. 96 - 100. *Photo:- H.C.Casserley*

crews were again subject to the rigours of downhill running, tender first with only a tarpaulin for protection and it has been said that few Blair Atholl locomen of this period lived long enough to retire. Caledonian 0-4-4Ts were to be found but they do not seem to have ever had adequate water capacity for regular work on the hill. From 1955 one or two LMS and BR 2-6-4Ts arrived and proved extremely popular.

For most of the LMS and BR era Blair Atholl was regarded as an outstation, a 'sub shed' of Perth but it contrived to maintain a fairly constant allocation. Apart from the banking, most of the local passenger trains were worked from the Blair Atholl end, usually by 4-4-0s, and five were on the complement at 1st July

towards the end of 1960 the Blair Atholl bankers represented almost the sum total of steam working on the Highland line. Even then a J39 or a pair of LMS 4F 0-6-0s could turn up at the shed, but soon afterwards it had more or less gone out of use, little more than a signing-on point for DMU drivers. Diesel operation had made banking unnecessary not because the new locomotives had greater power than the Class 5s but because double-heading, using a pair of Type 2s in multiple, applied from the start, almost universally to passenger trains and to a number of freight workings.

The shed appears not to have been finally abandoned, officially at least, until 1962. It still stands (May 1989).

25th January 1958. It will not be necessary to note the severity of Highland winters; most years a plough was necessary somewhere and it was a matter of everyday practice to have an engine so fitted at Blair Atholl. In the 1930s a Barney 0-6-0 with a medium plough was provided most winters but 4F 0-6-0s were used in the latter years. Behind the huge steel plough (above) lurks 4F No. 44254. *Photo:- J.L.Stevenson*

Blair Atholl, south end, in August 1948. The shed lacked for almost every amenity, though this was a feature it shared with most HR sheds. One of the few references in the very bare Highland Minutes relates to 'Engine Pit, Blair Atholl ......Estimate £50 .....Approved' (for once), on 7th December 1898. After that there is nothing. A simple coaling shelter was put up, very probably as a routine measure, when Government funds were available and there were two tanks, presumably provided at different periods as demand increased, or to overcome summer drought. Both were of 21,500 gallons capacity with the supply pumped from the Banvie Burn. *Photo:- J.L.Stevenson*

The decaying shell of Blair Atholl shed required comprehensive renewal by the late 'forties and the old Highland roof with its dormer and venting gave way to a spartan corrugated construction which sat ill upon the Highland stonework. 2-6-4Ts, usually of the Fairburn variety could increasingly be found as the 1950s drew to a close but BR engine No. 80126 (above) was a familiar resident by 1959. It had been about the area since at least 1956, delivered along with 80123, 80124 and 80125 to work scattered and unusual services in odd parts of Scotland. 80126 went to banking duties straight away, interspersed with 'frequent journeys' to Perth with passenger trains'. *Photo:- H.I.Cameron*

2-6-0 No. 77009 on 14th July 1954, one of the Standard 3MT series little known (until one ventured on to the Southern Region at the very last) outside the north of England and Scotland. In theory they were ideally suited to the Highland, an axleload which enabled them to work almost anywhere and yet with power enough for locals, goods and banking. In practice, they 'fell between two stools', if a locomotive can do such a thing. Their numbers were so few, particularly in the vastness of the Scottish Region that they remained unfamiliar to crews and sheds; called upon for class 4 and class 2 duties inevitably too much was asked of them a large part of the time. The diesels were more truly versatile and made light of the bank; double heading, on single engine loads, was after all employed throughout. Two BR 2-6-4Ts were still at Blair in 1960 but Type 2 diesels were working most of the trains. They would have been banked more through habit than necessity. Until the last year or so at least the shed still stood, mute and derelict. *Photo:- W.T.Stubbs*

Dingwall on 25th June 1949 with 0-4-4T No. 15199, the regular pilot at that time. The shed was remarkable not only for its striking outline (that steep pitch was unmistakable, and was presumably designed to avoid undue snow accumulation) but for its survival to the end of steam without replacement becoming necessary, through fire, storm or any of the other calamities visited upon Highland sheds.   *Photo:- J.L.Stevenson*

Dingwall

As junction for the Skye line (opened to Strome Ferry in 1870 and throughout to Kyle of Lochalsh only in 1897) Dingwall was assured of some considerable importance; in anticipation of this tenders were accepted on 4th October 1869 . . . . . . 'for Engine Shed, turntable foundations and two Gatehouses at Dingwall'. The shed was of wooden construction with a high pitched roof and stood at the south of the station and goods yard by 'Greenhill Cottage'. From the plan quite clearly a two road building, there is nevertheless some evidence to suggest that only one track was put in at first. The turntable, originally of 42 ft., was enlarged to 43 ft. 6 ins. between 1887 and 1890 but evidently fell upon evil days; it was never subsequently enlarged and appears to have been taken out of use about 1930. A 50 ft. 'table was available at Muir of Ord, only some six miles southward. Dingwall shed was very similar to that at Strome Ferry, built at the same time. The working of the line had at first to be entrusted to the 5 ft. 0 ins. 2-4-0s with rigid wheelbase ill suited to the curves and this led to the conversion of two of the Seafield class from 2-4-0 to 4-4-0. These would just have fitted the Dingwall turntable as would No. 70, the first of the 5 ft. 3½ ins. Skye Bogies which came out in 1882 with a 41 ft. 6 ins. wheelbase. Later

members of the class, which emerged between 1892 and 1901, had longer tenders for which the above-mentioned extension of the Dingwall table was necessary.

Services between Dingwall and Strome Ferry in early days were far from intensive; in February 1878 for example, the timetable showed only a single (mixed) train in each direction but from about 1880 the pattern was of two trains in winter and three in summer, one at least being mixed. Things improved further with the opening to Kyle in November 1897 and three of the four services now ran through from and to Inverness, a change which must have marked something of a decline in the importance of Dingwall shed. However, the Strathpeffer branch had been opened in 1885, diverging from the Skye line at Fodderty Junction, and for this Dingwall was at first provided with the 2-2-2T No. 12 (to which reference has been made under Aberfeldy). Subsequently in 1890 this was replaced by the new Jones 0-4-4ST No. 13 which stayed until 1901, when Yankee Tank No. 51 arrived. In 1905 the new Drummond 0-4-4T No. 25 took up a long residence at Dingwall until 1930, occasionally relieved by a 4-4-0T or even a Lochgorm 0-6-0T with Nos. 15017 and 16118 respectively recorded. There was an exciting interlude in the

Skye Bogie No. 33 (LMS No. 14283) at Dingwall. Nine of these famous engines (in terms of railway romance the equivalent of the Skye Boat Song.......) were built between 1882 and 1901; the last, extraordinarily, did not go until 1930 and in LMS livery they appeared impossibly ancient. Straths and Small Bens supplemented the Skye Bogies on the Kyle line, though there were still two at Dingwall, along with a Small Ben and an 0-4-4T, in 1919.   *Photo:- R.D.Stephen*

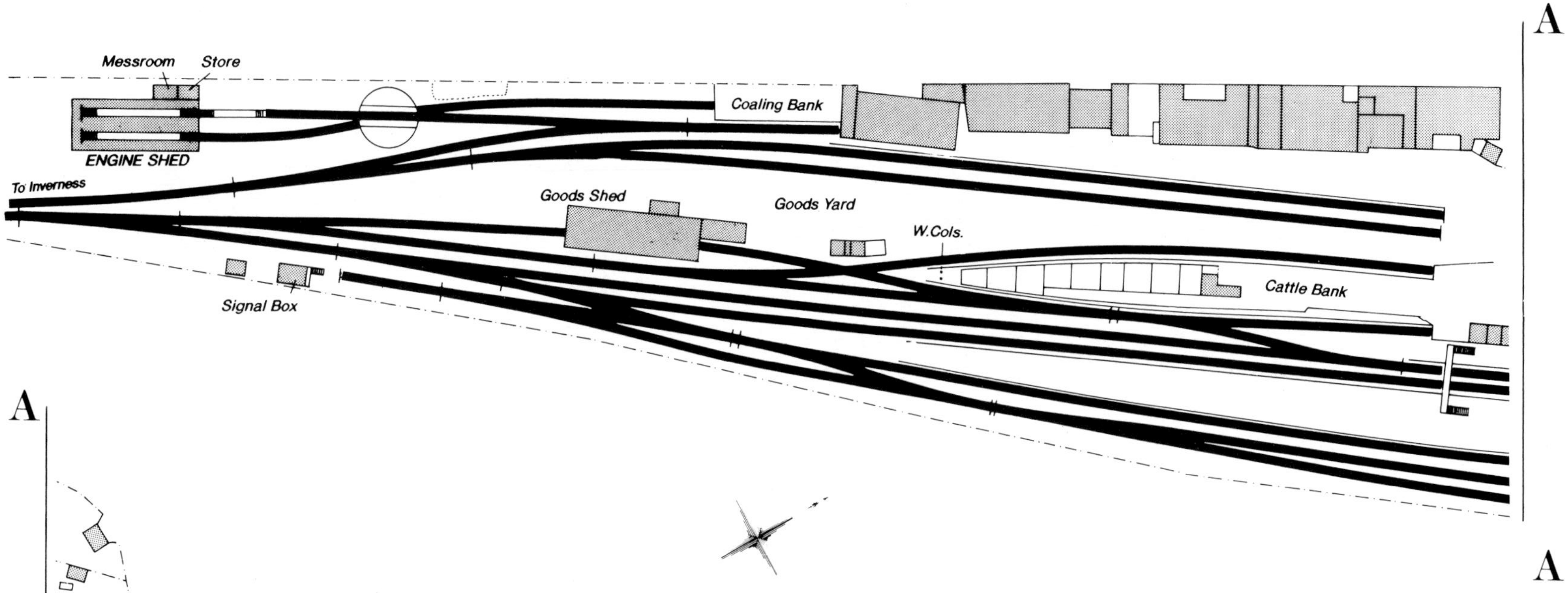

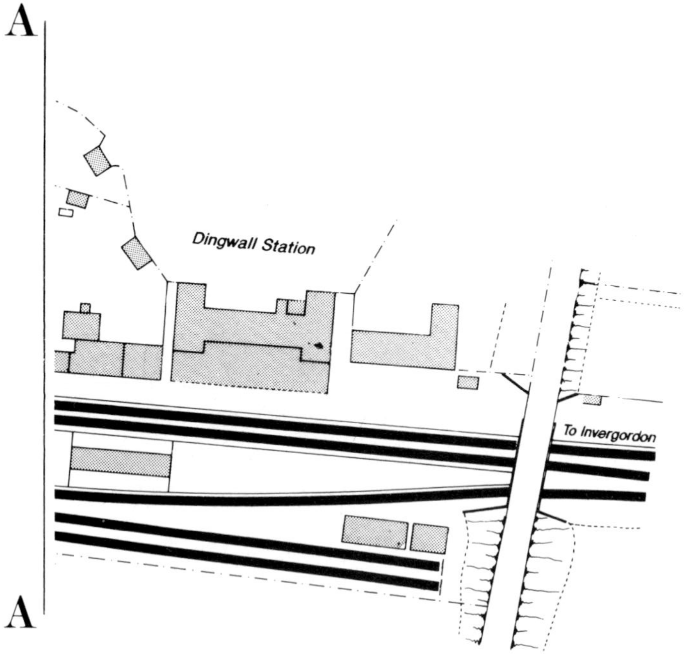

Dingwall in 1904. The shed was much like its contemporaries elsewhere on the Highland, close by the station amidst self-contained arrangements for goods, locomotive servicing, passenger traffic, p.w. and anything else. Despite its often perilous finances the Highland 'opened up' tracts of Britain like no other line. Much of the road system was single, with passing spaces, into the 1950s and 60s and the passing of a day [Sundays excepted] was marked for years by the train. Any luxury, and many essentials, a long awaited letter or parcel depended on the railway, to a degree beyond that experienced in most parts of Britain.

Messroom
Store
ENGINE SHED
To Inverness
Coaling Bank
Goods Yard
Goods Shed
Signal Box
W.Cols.
Cattle Bank

A
A

Dingwall Station
To Invergordon
A
A

Dingwall on 24th September 1935. It had begun life as a busy junction shed but in early LMS days through working of the 'Skye Line' had become usual and its importance waned. Responsibility began a shift from the Kyle trains to the wholly humdrum (by comparison) Strathpeffer branch.   *Photo:- W.A.Camwell*

Dingwall, 8th August 1935, No. 14404 *Ben Clebrig*. Despite a decline into relative somnolence 'main line' engines could usually be found at the shed for there was all manner of work to be done locally as well as banking. Nevertheless by 1935 the official complement had been reduced to only three, ex - CR 0-4-4T No. 15226 Barney 0-6-0 No. 17695 and Cumming Goods 4-6-0 No. 17951.

Photo:- H.N.James

late 1920s when the LMS tried various exotic forms of power on the branch, one at least of the G & SW 0-4-4Ts of the 305 class, No. 16081, a Sentinel steam railcar and, even more extraordinary, LNW 0-6-2T No. 7727. After 1930 Yankee Tanks Nos. 15013 and 15014 appeared until withdrawn in 1934 and thereafter tender engines were used, usually a Barney 0-6-0. Passenger services to Strathpeffer ceased in March 1946.

During the 1914-1918 War there was a very great increase in freight traffic over the Kyle line and the Skye Bogies were supplemented by larger 4-4-0s and by

the struggle and instead a couple of Superheated Goods would have been found overnight. During the 1939-1945 War naval traffic again came into prominence and sidings were laid in at Fodderty Junction for the storage of wagons for the mine traffic. No. 14392 *Loch Naver* was regularly at Dingwall from 1940 until 1947 and did much work banking trains to Raven's Rock and making freight trips to Invergordon. A Caledonian 0-4-4T also arrived and stayed until about 1960 as shunting pilot. The Loch was replaced by a Caledonian 4-4-0, e.g. No. M14487 which was on the Strathpeffer goods in June 1949 and

Dingwall on 2nd July 1961. Ex - CR locomotives generally monopolised the British Railways period - by 1950 the allocation stood at only two, 4-4-0 No. 54487 and 0-4-4T No. 55199. On 7th July 1955 4-4-0 No. 54493 was banking Kyle trains up to Ravens Rock and No 54458 'was at the shed, in steam'. *Photo:- W.T.Stubbs*

some of the 'foreign' classes on loan to the Highland. The traffic rose to a peak in 1918 when no fewer than four trains were timetabled daily from Kyle to Belleport Admiralty sidings betwween Alness and Invergordon, the public making do with a single mixed train. Dingwall shed would no doubt have been heavily involved in providing for these workings which were mainly concerned with the movement of naval mines.

The allocation of 1919 shows two Skye Bogies and a Small Ben at Dingwall together with No. 25, but by the end of the 1920s the Skye Bogies had at last given up

No. 54463 was here also. The 0-4-4T eventually gave way to a Western Region 0-6-0 pannier tank, one of two previously at Dornoch, and No. 1649 of this class was shunting at Dingwall in July 1961, the last regular steam working north of Inverness.

The Dingwall pilot was withdrawn ' about the end of 1961' and the shed was closed and demolished. The site is now occupied by a garage.

Locomotive Magazine, 10th August 1919, and Tatlow, *Highland Locomotives*, OPC.

The shed on 21st June 1960, appearing hardly the worse for wear after some ninety years of use. Only the peculiar *internal* bracing seems to indicate some deterioration in the structure.

Photo:- W.A.Camwell

By the mid 1920s Small Bens and Lochs had become regular performers on the Kyle line, working out of Inverness during the summer months. With track improvements the Cumming 4-6-0 Goods appeared around 1928, handling most trains until replaced by class 5s in 1946. These types would turn up at Dingwall most days on some sort of work, a situation which continued into BR days with 5MT 4-6-0s and ex-CR 4-4-0s. The last engine was reported to be a Western Region 0-6-0 pannier tank - 'it shunts at Dingwall and is the only steam locomotive working in the Northern Highlands.' This would be late 1961 or even early 1962; very soon afterwards the shed was declared to be 'disconnected'

Photo:- P. J. Kelley

The classic, if familiar Dornoch portrait, one of the very few early engine shed photographs which can be considered 'the perfect study'. From *The Locomotive* : *The County Town of Dornoch was left some 7 miles from the railway, the connection being supplied by a coach which plied to and from the railway station at The Mound. This means of conveyance was somewhat inconvenient and towards the end of the century, the desire to obtain better railway communication began to grow in the district. The Highland when approached declared themselves in favour of the scheme and on August 13th 1898, agreed to work the line, the company remaining nominally independent until the grouping.* Photo:- C.Brown

Dornoch

The 7¾ mile Dornoch Light Railway opened from The Mound, some 80 miles north of Inverness, in June 1902 and despite its title was constructed largely to conventional standards. The underbridges though few were lightly built and an axle loading limit of 12 tons applied. The small wooden engine shed, a typical Highland product resting on a dwarf brick wall with wooden tank outside, would have opened at the same time.

For the opening the Highland required of course an engine with light axle load and sent up one of the three Lochgorm Tanks, No.56, at first named *Balnain* but for its new command renamed *Dornoch*. It worked regularly until 1905 when the Drummond 0-4-4 tanks began to appear and more or less monopolised the line until the last was withdrawn in 1957. No.56 was however, back at Dornoch for a time about 1919. All four of the 0-4-4Ts, Nos. 25, 40, 45 and 46 (LMS Nos. 15051-4), were there at one time or another. Although Dornoch was an outstation of Inverness, up to national-isation maintenance seems usually to have been carried

out at Helmsdale; after 1948 the latter was given a separate code, 60C, with Dornoch and Tain as sub sheds.

Old age and infirmity began to overtake the Highland tanks and after 1945 only two remained to work the line, Nos.15051 and 15053. Long absences occurred in St.Rollox Works as no spare boiler was available and No.15053 lay out of use at Dornoch for some months in 1948. With considerable ingenuity one always seemed to be available but upon withdrawal of No. 15051 in June 1956 a Caledonian 0-4-4T, No.55236 and with an axle loading of 18 tons far too heavy, had to be pressed into service, deputising for 55053 in August. Calamitously, 55053 broke a coupled axle in December and never ran again, being withdrawn in January 1957. 2MT 2-6-0s appeared for a time but by the following April two 16XX pannier tanks had been summoned from the Western Region. Nos. 1646 and 1649 worked the line very competently for the remaining three years, No. 1649 heading the last train on 11th. June 1960.

Rain at Dornoch. *The Locomotive* **again** : *The railway was opened for traffic on June 2nd, 1902. Although theoretically a light railway, the line was very substantially built, and differed but little from the main line. The Board of Trade impo-sed many restrictions, which resulted in a much heavier expenditure than would otherwise have been necessary. Unlike many light railways, the line was fenced throughout, and gates were provided at the numerous level crossings.*

Photo:- P.J.Garland

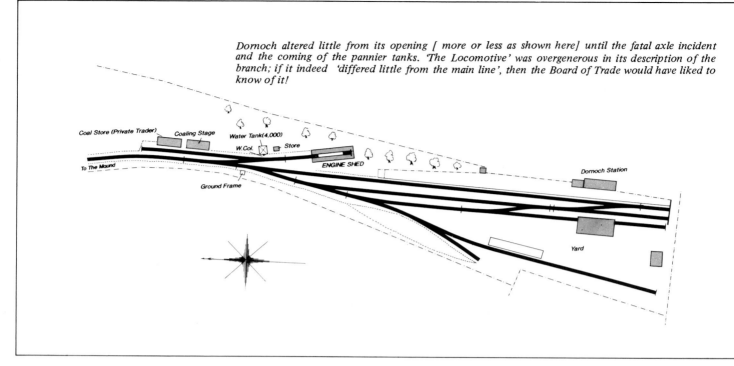

Dornoch altered little from its opening [more or less as shown here] until the fatal axle incident and the coming of the pannier tanks. 'The Locomotive' was overgenerous in its description of the branch; if it indeed 'differed little from the main line', then the Board of Trade would have liked to know of it!

No. 15053 on 11th June 1936. The sturdy little shed had a thoroughly homely air about it, an impression emphasised by the tiny Highland tanks, increasingly unusual as ex - CR 0-4-4Ts (then regarded as a rather dull 'standard' type [!]) carried out much of the branch work elsewhere. On many pilgrimages north in the 1930s and 1950s Dornoch was an essential stopping place and its qualities drew various charming descriptions. *The Railway Observer* noted No. 15052 'preparing for its nights rest' in 1928 and in 1937 15053 was similarly occupied : *The 0-4-4 tank 15053 works the Dornoch Light Railway; it was observed, neatly shedded, in the evening, and on the 9. 10 a.m. train the next morning. According to the engine crew, this little machine has its boiler washed out once a fortnight, and goes to Inverness about every four months.*
Photo:- W.A.Camwell

55051 on 22nd May 1952; Dornoch was now if anything even more of a fascination. Nestling among trees the everyday work of a vanished era seemed to be acted out utterly heedless of World Wars, Depression, Austerity and the Decline of Empire. The *wooden* tank held 4000 gallons and the drivers' dwelling house stood at the end of the coal siding.

Photo:- W.A.Camwell

55051 on 10th September 1953. A final breakdown brought about the demise of the Highland tanks, described by 'River Tay' in *The Railway Magazine* of April 1957 : ......*the withdrawal of No. 55053 was precipitated by an alarming mishap; while working a mixed train from Dornoch to The Mound the leading axle broke, and one of the wheels careered along the ballast before coming into contact with a lineside gatepost. Fortunately, the train was not derailed. Restricted axle weights made its replacement a matter of some difficulty, and its place was eventually taken by a Western Region pannier tank, No. 1646. The new arrival was transferred from Croes Newydd and is the first locomotive of the Western Region to be transferred to Scotland. It left Wales on February 7, marshalled into a goods train, and reached Helmsdale of which Dornoch is a sub-depot four days later.* Photo:- Brian Hilton

Forres in 1934. It was originally intended that the line south to Aviemore and Perth should start from Nairn, some distance west of Forres. It was subsequently determined that the line (Inverness and Perth Jct. Rly.) should begin from Forres, which required a realignment to make the triangular junction. The shed lay on the old alignment and drawings of 1863 show the Inverness and Perth Co. as owners. *Photo: C. Brown collection.*

Forres

The original, through, station at Forres was opened in 1858 by the Inverness and Aberdeen Junction Railway. A junction was established in 1863, on opening of the Inverness and Perth Junction Railway and a new station built some 200 yards south of the old one, on a sharp curve. A triangle was thereby formed with the new line to the south and in the same year a two road stone built shed was put up, close by the old alignment. The tender of Messrs Squair & Mackintosh, £2313, was accepted on 20th May 1863, for 'Forres Station House, Engine House for four Engines, Water Tank and Turntable'.

The building indeed held four engines, its two roads of 99ft each originally graced by a pair of archways, removed around 1910 and wooden screening and girder supports substituted. A turntable was provided, shown as 44ft 8ins in 1881 and engines at times certainly used the triangle. Most companies contented themselves with turntables of conventional diameter, 42ft to 46ft, 50ft and upwards as engines grew in size. The Highland (or at least its records in this regard) was concerned with much more precise dimensions. The Forres 'table was listed as 50ft 3ins by 1901 and 48ft 6ins by 1920, presumably a record of the varied home grown bits of extension rail got from Inverness, a blacksmith no doubt, from the works - Lochgorm Smithy. By 1948 the size was determined at a conventional and perhaps nominal 50ft. This still meant most 4-6-0s were forced to use the triangle; the 'table was overlong for a Ben but too short for a Castle.

Many different workings were attended to at Forres and Jones saw to the provision of dormitory accommodation. This he made known on 21st July 1895, with customary directness (and economy-it is the same as that issued for Blair) of manner :

Notice
Dormitory at Forres

This Dormitory has been specially fitted up for the benefit of Enginemen and Firemen who may be Stationed at Forres as Spare men, and will also be for the use of Enginemen and Firemen arriving at Forres and having time to rest themselves but not having sufficient time at their disposal to look for lodgings elsewhere. It must be distinctly understood that the Dormitory will be used solely as a bedroom for the benefit of those requiring it. It must be kept as clean as circumstances permit

It will be under the charge of the Loco Foreman and will be locked when not in use.

Should any damage be done to any portion thereof by any of the occupants during his stay he will be held responsible for cost of repairs.

[signed]   D   Jones,   Locomotive Engineer.

A Duke 4-4-0 (Lochgorm Bogie Series) No. 73 *Rosehaugh* inside Forres. The complement, particularly in HR days presented a spectacular variety of engine power and of the 1919 allocation two, the Duke No. 67 and a 2-4-0 No. 27B of 1863 had been the last survivors of their classes for over ten years. *Photo: J.L. Stevenson collection.*

Forres on 10th June 1936, long after its original arches had been removed. At the shed was 14380 *Loch Ness*, standard 3F tank No. 16623, 14406 *Ben Slioch*, 14408 *Ben Hope* and 0-6-0 No. 17698. *Photo: W.A. Camwell.*

The shed at Forres lay in a triangle in a fairly open site despite the gradual crowding of saw mills, Engineers sleeper creosoting shop, flour mill, a 'chemical works' even, and of the station itself. Nevertheless, it was a poor layout; there were points at the very shed entrance, an open coal stage, and the Highland could afford to neglect the turntable. *Photo: W.A. Camwell.*

Forres was responsible for much of the train working between Inverness and Keith, a relatively easy stretch of line apart from Mulben bank near Keith, 2½ miles at 1 in 60 against eastbound trains. 2-4-0s were mainly used until the turn of the century, replaced gradually by 4-4-0s. The 1919 allocation showed a Small Ben, four Straths, a Clyde Bogie and a Duke together with an 0-6-4 Banking Tank, a 4-4-0T spare for Burghead and an old 2-4-0 as snow plough and ballast engine. A further Ben was outstationed at Keith.

By the 1930s half a dozen Small Bens, a Big Ben two Lochs, two Barneys and two standard 0-6-0Ts formed the usual complement, the last Banking Tank leaving Forres in 1935. These particular engines were provided mainly for assistance to Dava, 15 miles mainly at 1 in 75, work later taken over by a 4-4-0. A Standard Tank shunted the yard, No. 16623, and another of the class was outbased at Burghead. These two were replaced by a couple of Caledonian 0-6-0 tanks in 1940, Nos. 16299 and 16301, transferred from Grangemouth. Another incomer was CR 0-4-4T No. 15220 which arrived for a short stay in 1939, usually making a freight trip to Elgin and shunting there. In 1950 No. 55178 of the same class appeared and stayed until withdrawal in 1958.

Assistance to Dava took place from early days, the Working Timetables of the 1890s showing eight banking trips to Dava and two to Grantown which at that time had a turntable. 2-4-0s would have been the engines mainly involved but the older 4-4-0s often piloted passenger

trains as far as Dalwhinnie or Dalnaspidal. With the opening of the Aviemore Direct line in 1898 such workings were reduced but the two through freights to Perth were regularly assisted until closure of the Dava line in 1965. Normally the assisting engine was on the rear of a freight train but was coupled ahead of a passenger train. It was supposed to come off at Dava but as this was a little short of the summit the assisting engine may have continued at the rear for a little further, although there was no banking key.

An exception to the 4-4-0s was No. 14675 *Taymouth Castle* which spent the summers of 1937, to 1939 at Forres, its main task to work the 5.10pm to Aviemore, a heavy train which conveyed sleeping cars to Kings Cross and Euston. On the Inverness - Keith line the work of the shed with its small Bens was of a good standard and some quite smart running was required. Towards the end of the 1930s some of the turns were taken over by Class 5s.

By 1941 three CR Saturated Dunalastair 4-4-0s had appeared at Forres, Nos. 14332, 14333 and 14337. They were not in the best of condition but were capable of some of the lighter turns to Elgin and Keith. Perhaps the most interesting arrival was No. 14385 *Loch Tay* which worked regularly at Forres on passenger and freight turns from 1941 until its withdrawal as the last of its class in 1950. The Small Bens were moved to the North line although No. 14406 *Ben Slioch* remained at Forres during most of the war years. This period saw ex-

14391 *Loch Shin* inside Forres. At the rear of the shed a sort of lean-to was tacked on, rendering it a single-ended type of building. This was presumably not original (see drawing p.46) and its purpose is unclear. *Photo: J.L. Stevenson collection.*

The clutter surrounding Forres engine shed, No. 39 running westward with a short rake of wagons. The date is apparently June 1906 and the volume of traffic, for an obscure Highland town, and despite the HR's relatively low levels of activity in this regard, demonstrates how absolutely such places were dependent upon the railway. *Photo: J.L. Stevenson collection.*

ceptionally heavy traffic and LMS 2-8-0s were among the unusual engines to turn up at Forres. The Second World War is nicely recalled by the late W McGowan Gradon BA (also responsible for an early history of the Furness Railway - see Volume IV) in a Railway World article of 1954. In the autumn and winter of 1943 - 44 Forres housed 'a motley collection, the Highland represented by *Loch Tay* (14385) and *Ben Slioch* (14406)'. The former usually concerned itself with the Burghead - Hopeman branch (it would totter off to Elgin around 9am) whilst the Ben was often on the Dava banking duties. Large scale manoeuvres in anticipation of D Day took place in the spring of 1944, thousands of troops with hundreds of tanks. These were loaded on 'warwells' to 75 tons, headed by a pair of 8F 2-8-0s and assisted with doubtful advantage by the wheezing *Ben Slioch* . Ex-Caledonian 0-6-0Ts Nos. 16299 and 16301 coped with the increased shunting load; one spent the entire day so engaged, the other travelling to Nairn to shunt and work goods on the Fort George branch. Freight to Keith was handled by a Barney 0-6-0 and some trains, Inverness - Perth were sent via Forres to relieve congestion over Slochd Summit. Perth during this time also supplied 8Fs for goods, the heaviest turn, the 10.25pm through Perth job 'made up in the early afternoon in the loop behind the Aviemore line down platform'. Ex-

CR 4-4-0s principally for the passenger traffic to Keith despite being 'pretty decrepit' nevertheless found occasional employment on banking up to Dava.

By 1945 No. 14410 *Ben Dearg* was at Forres and No. 14678 *Gordon Castle* from about 1943 until its withdrawal in 1946. The two Forres Barneys were eventually replaced by Caledonian 3F 0-6-0s, Nos.17591 and 17620, while Pickersgill 4-4-0s began to arrive in 1947, Nos. 14472, 14473, 14481, and 14482. A 350hp shunter,

14406 *Ben Slioch*. The Forres tank, with locally fashioned roofing, held 18,040 gallons. *Photo: J. Hooper collection.*

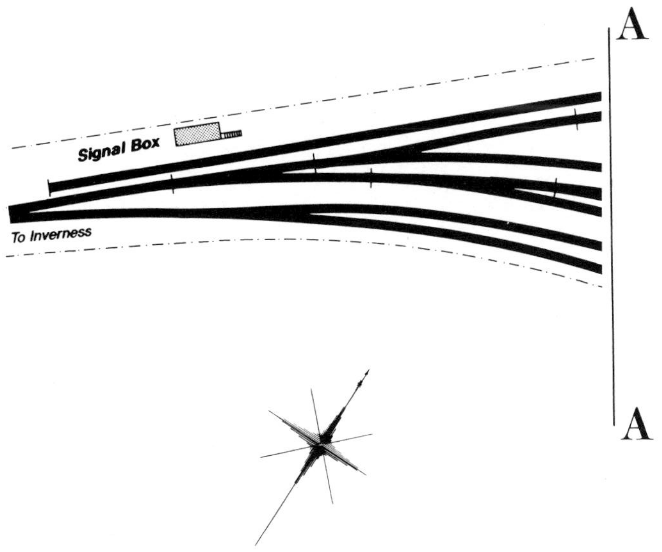

The Highland shed at Forres. It lay in a broad triangle as the text relates and it is unfortunate that space does not allow its varied detail to be shown. All manner [see p40] of activity went on within its crowded confines; works and stores [it would be termed an industrial estate today], punctuated by the regular traffic of trains and light engines. The text also makes reference to the disposition of the shed layout - the site had every advantage of space when the shed was built but the old Inverness and Perth Junction Co. contrived a studiedly awkward and inconvenient arrangement. This ancient muddle apparently survived until the end even when Forres acquired an importance relatively 'national' in character. Its finest [documented] moments seem to have come in the Second World War; it had been elevated to '29K' by the LMS and by 19th October 1942 had three CR 4-4-0s, Nos. 14332, 14333 and 14337, four HR engines, Barneys Nos. 17698 and 17704, 'Ben Slioch' and 'Loch Tay' and standard tanks Nos 16299 and 16301. Its total 'equivalent booked engine turn - 7' was less than remarkable but warranted the classification 'Secret' [a downgrading - 'Most' had been neatly deleted].

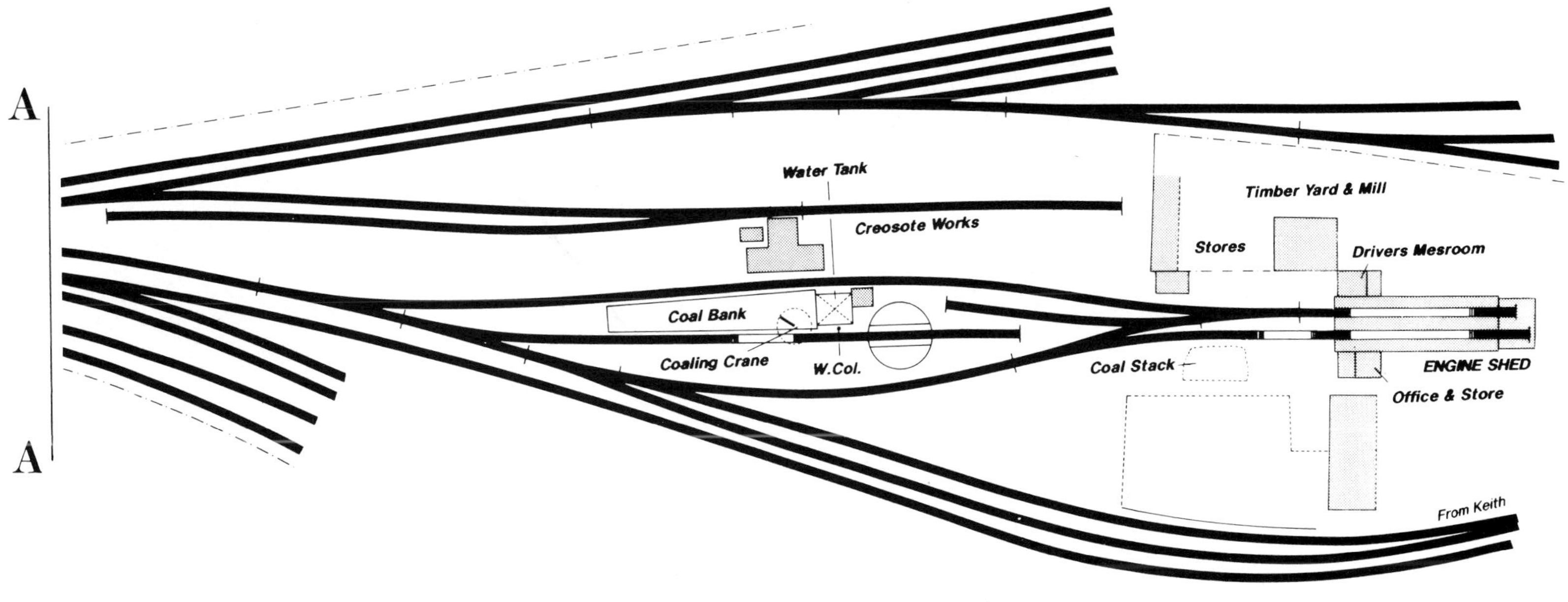

A
A

A
A

Signal Box

To Inverness

Water Tank

Creosote Works

Coal Bank

Coaling Crane

W.Col.

Timber Yard & Mill

Stores

Drivers Messroom

Coal Stack

ENGINE SHED

Office & Store

From Keith

A
A

Improvements were effected to the coaling arrangements at Forres, again most likely a consequence of wartime pressures. An ancient upright swivel crane had long been in use (see p.38), to be replaced by this more robust (though doubtless second-hand) example and a simple shelter. *Photo: J. Hooper collection.*

Caledonian tank No. 55178 enjoying the modern Forres facilities in August 1954. *Photo: J.L. Stevenson.*

Forres on 26th May 1930. The Strath 4-4-0s were gone by the end of that year but the complement still held great interest. By June 1935 there were two Lochs, *Ness* and *Shin*, seven Small Bens, *Alder, Wyvis, More, Vrackie, Armin, Slioch and Hope,* a Large Ben, 14422, *Ben a 'Chaoruinn,* two standard 0-6-0Ts Nos. 16415 and 16623, a Banking Tank No. 15300 and a Barney, 0-6-0 No. 17704.   *Photo:- H. C. Casserley*

Forres on 1st May 1936. Inside the shed were 4-4-0s 14399 *Ben Wyvis*, 14400 *Ben More* and 14422 *Ben a'Chaoruinn*, all Forres engines and outside two standard locos, 0-6-0 No. 4317 and 4-6-0 No. 5165, both of Perth. Other Forres engines about the yard were 14391 *Loch Shin*, 14398, *Ben Alder* and 14408, *Ben Hope*. A standard 0-6-0T , No. 16415, was awaiting despatch to St Rollox. *Photo: E.W. Hannan*.

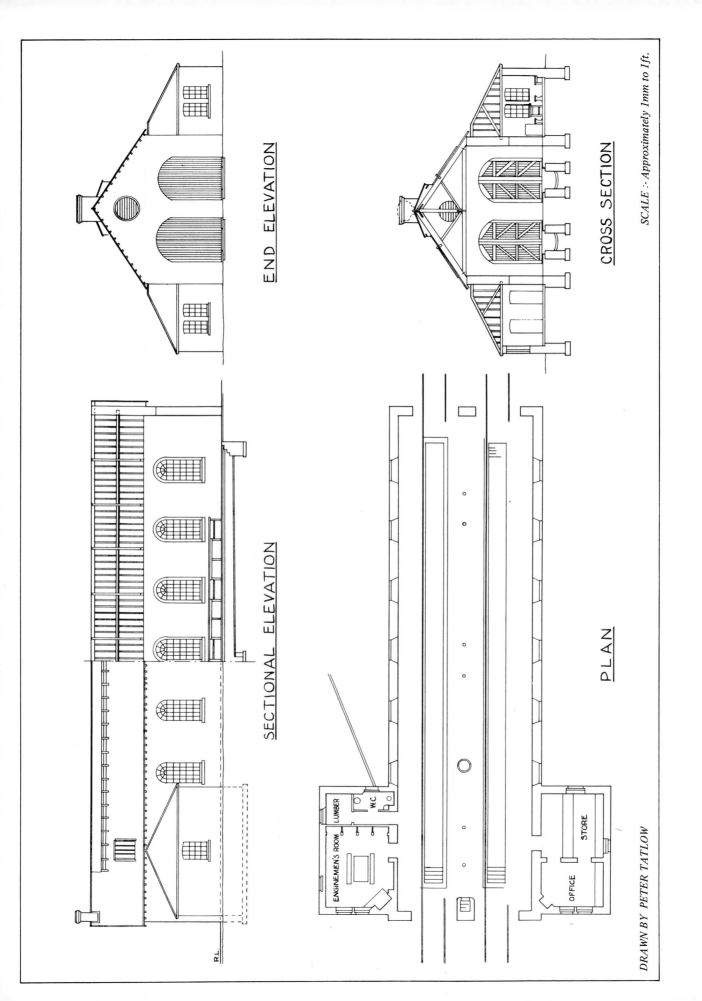

END ELEVATION

CROSS SECTION

SCALE :- *Approximately 1mm to 1ft.*

SECTIONAL ELEVATION

R.L.

PLAN

ENGINEMEN'S ROOM

LUMBER

W.C.

STORE

OFFICE

DRAWN BY PETER TATLOW

'The Diesel' at Forres on 23rd May 1959. Its arrival allowed the 0-6-0Ts to be disposed of, which left only a handful of active steam engines (by 1947 they had declined to just seven, *Ben Dearg* and *Loch Tay*, CR 4-4-0s No. 14473 and 14481, 3F 0-6-0s Nos. 17591 and 17620, and 3F tank No. 16301), soon to be displaced by DMUs. Closure had been under consideration in 1956 but was deferred for the highly novel reason (by more recent lights) 'that skilled older men would not care to move. and thus be lost to the railway service'. *Photo: J. L. Stevenson*

Forres in its last years, in June 1960. The crumbling wooden gable is a contrast to its ornate arched origins.
Photo:- R.M.Casserley

D3735, took over from the CR 0-6-0Ts in 1959.

The introduction of DMUs on the Inverness - Aberdeen service in 1959 took much of the work away from Forres; an official closure date of May 1962 has been recorded but the likelihood is that it lingered on for another year or more as a stabling/signing on point, until closure of the Dava line. D3735 was transferred from 'Forres, 60E' to Inverness in January 1964.

The sentiments of 1956 could never long survive the ceaseless press of economy; the shed closed finally around 1962. By June 1963 it was derelict. *Photo: W.T. Stubbs.*

15199 at Fort George on 25th September 1935. This sort of wooden shed has come to typify the Highland above all other companies, possibly through the near ubiquitous smoke 'pot', once described, not entirely in jest, as a 'gothic wood'.
Photo: W.A. Camwell.

Fort George. There is every liklehood that this shed closed shortly before 1947 but this has been impossible to devine beyond doubt [see text]. It is for that a fine plan and a story of great interest. The LMS had an awkward habit, various departments issuing 'lists' of 'Motive Power Depots'. They usually failed to get even every spelling right, and Fort George's dogged inclusion to 1947 and beyond might well be a flight of fancy, or an accounting dodge.

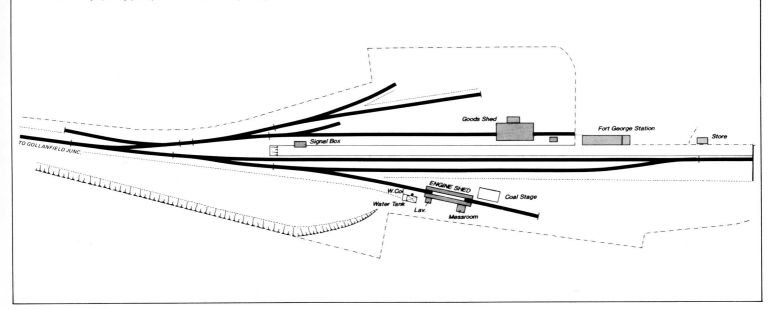

Fort George

The Fort George branch, only 1¾ miles in length, was opened in July 1899 ostensibly to serve the military depot of that name on the Moray Firth, but stopping as it did some two miles short of its stated objective most of the traffic came from the small village of Ardersier, close to the station. The branch started at Gollanfield Junction (formerly named Fort George) 8½ miles east of Inverness. The shed opened with the branch; a neat wooden structure designed to hold a single tank engine it stood opposite the station platform. A wooden water tank adjoined it.

Branch services started with a Lochgorm 0-6-0 tank, No. 16 suitably named *Fort George*, and this remained the regular engine for a few years. Thereafter Inverness appears to have sent out whatever they had

available. 2-4-0 No. 29 *Raigmore* was recorded about 1910 and soon afterwards 0-4-4T No. 45 made an appearance. But later tender engines were the rule; Small Bens, Lochs and even a Skye Bogie were used, although a standard 0-6-0T No. 16416 was there in 1928, having a break from its shunting duties at Inverness.

In 1935 regular operation by tank engines recommenced when Caledonian 0-4-4T No. 15226 arrived; occasionally relieved by No. 15199, it could normally be found at Fort George until 3rd April 1944, when it headed the last passenger train made up on this occasion to two coaches instead of the usual one. The shed probably closed at this time but remained 'officially open', an accounting device perhaps, in several LMS listings of 1947.

Fort George in August 1937 with ex-CR 0-4-4T No. 15226. From *The Locomotive* of 14th August 1915: *Fort George Branch . . . . .designed to afford more convenient access to the military depot at Fort George, from which the station of that name was some four miles distant. A branch 1¾ miles in length, was therefore made from the old Fort George Station to the village of Ardersier and was opened on July 1st 1899. The terminal station of this branch was named Fort George and the old station of that name was henceforth known as Gollanfield Junction. Both line and shed were built by Messrs. George Sutherland.* **Operated as an outstation of Inverness Fort George was built in period Highland fashion, a solid wooden building providing secure overnight resting place for a single branch tank. Coal was stacked on the simple open platform at the rear and ashes simply dumped round about. The branch ran through flat country but there was a sharp rise and reverse curves approaching the terminus. The train made about eleven trips daily, some mixed and there were late services on a Saturday. For a time an afternoon run was made into Inverness and back.** *Photo: J.L. Stevenson.*

The original shed at Fortrose, 24th September 1935. The engine is 14381 *Loch Ericht*. The 4-4-0 Yankee Tanks had seen considerable service in Highland days but latter years, particularly the LMS period, brought a variety of tender engines. It was after all a lengthy branch. *Photo: W.A. Camwell.*

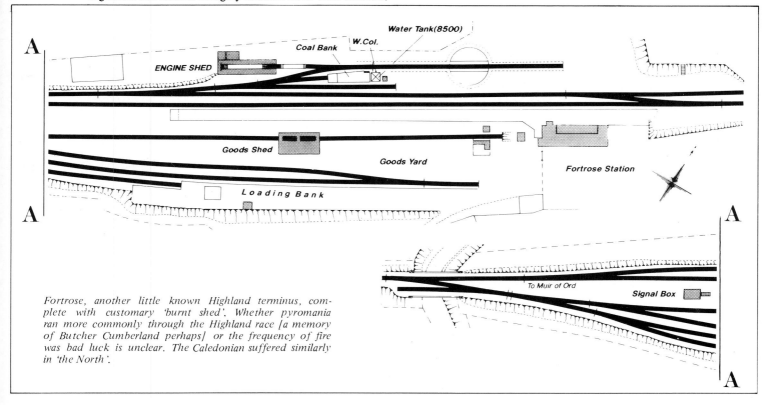

Fortrose, another little known Highland terminus, complete with customary 'burnt shed'. Whether pyromania ran more commonly through the Highland race [a memory of Butcher Cumberland perhaps] or the frequency of fire was bad luck is unclear. The Caledonian suffered similarly in 'the North'.

Fortrose

The large peninsula on the north side of the Beauly Firth known as the Black Isle was connected with Inverness by road over the Kessock Ferry, near the mouth of the River Ness, but the railway when it arrived in February 1894 approached from the west, from a junction with the North line at Muir of Ord.

The terminus of the branch was at Fortrose, some seven miles from Inverness as the crow flies but some four times this by rail. A shed was in use from the start, a single road wooden building with a lean-to structure on one side. There was a 50ft. turntable built by Cowans Sheldon dated 1896 and a similar 'table at Muir of Ord. In 1943 the shed was burnt down and its occupant, No. 14416 *Ben a' Bhuird* suffered damage externally which required it to be repainted. A replacement shed, largely constructed in corrugated iron and resembling an overgrown garage, was erected in its place and served until it was closed on the withdrawal of passenger services in October 1950. Neither shed appears to have been long enough to accommodate fully a tender engine.

The branch had some steep gradients and goods traffic could be quite heavy at times but the Yankee 4-4-0 tanks seem to have met requirements and more or less monopolised the line in Highland days. No. 15 (later 52) was there at the start before going to Fort Augustus. No.102 came there in 1910 and by 1919 No. 101. Perhaps the little known No. 51 was on the branch at times also. A surprise appearance around 1912 was that of 0-6-0T No. 23, these engines being vacuum fitted for a time about then. It must have been a short visit as the class could not have worked the line with any pretence of time-keeping.

By LMS days an interesting variety of tender engines began to take over from the tanks, the duty being one of the last performed by Clyde Bogie No. 81A *Colville* in August 1923. Skye Bogie No. 14277 was there in 1928 but the following year found *Ben Clebrig* and indeed the class largely monopolised the branch until about 1949. However, No. 14386 *Loch Tummel* was branch engine in June 1936 and a Barney 0-6-0 No. 17703 in August 1937. After 1948 Caledonian 4-4-0 engines appeared, No. 54439 in March 1949, but Highland locomotives returned with Superheated Goods No. 57956 in July and *Ben Wyvis* in August. CR 4-4-0 No. 54470 was at Fortrose in July 1950 but in October passenger services were taken off and the shed closed. Goods traffic continued until June 1960 usually worked by a CR 0-6-0 from Inverness.

14397 *Ben-y-Gloe* on the Fortrose branch train. The Black Isle enjoyed mild winters compared to much of the mountain country that surrounded it; the line was by no means as flat as its coastal location might suggest and a tender engine seems to have been required, for the often substantial freight traffic and to carry enough coal for a days work. Rain, wind and dust made turning at each end highly desirable.   *Photo:- W. A. Camwell*

No. 14399 *Ben Wyvis* at Fortrose in August 1948. The 'table was an ancient one, and needed cajoling, like many on the Highland but crews were prepared to make the considerable effort. *Photo: J.L. Stevenson.*

There was no balancing engine shed at Muir of Ord, the western end of the branch, so it was not possible to house the engine there, even if such a reordering was possible, after the unfortunate fire of 1943. The blistered *Ben a'Bhuird* was taken off to St.Rollox, Glasgow and its replacement stabled amidst the debris for a while. The new shed largely in corrugated iron, was put up with remarkable alacrity, given that it was also wartime. In England such a renewal would demand several years cogitation, a couple of reports and two or three site visits. The Highland section enjoyed a certain measure of independence, through its very remoteness. This, disdain for the south (which began at Perth, or even northwards thereof) and a keen appreciation of winter rigours, ensured that a replacement shed was up in months, if not weeks. *Photo: J. Hooper collection.*

14397 *Ben-y-Gloe* again, on 17th June 1947, reverses past the signal box, out of view, towards the engine shed. *Photo: W.A. Camwell*

The 'garage' at Fortrose, in a beam of sunshine (it is, essentially, the constant rain which is the beauty of the north of Scotland - it deters many people and without it the short sublime periods afterwards would not be). It would be within Highland tradition that any usable material from the old shed was incorporated in the new structure - what could be the old debris lies close by and slightly battered in the sunlight stands that familier smoke pot, 'gothic wood' preserved.
Photo:- J.L.Stevenson

The prospect northwards from the ancient confines of the Helmsdale engine shed. Few internal views of Highland sheds exist and this one conveniently shows the type of ventilation employed. The Highland did not employ the conventional troughing to carry off smoke (even at its only large straight shed, Perth) but relied on the cheaper expedient of a simple 'hood' for each locomotive - four, two or one, whatever number the particular building was designed for. It was inevitably less flexible and locos might be left wrongly positioned, with only the open central vent to exhaust the smoke.
Photo: J. Hooper collection.

Helmsdale

In June 1871 the North line reached Helmsdale, for three years the terminus whilst the final section was driven on across the endless moorland of Sutherland and Caithness. An engine shed was established from the beginning at Helmsdale, a convenient point both to start certain passenger and goods trains on their way and also to provide any assistance that might be required.

The first shed was built of timber, a two road structure with a steeply angled roof much after the fashion of the building at Dingwall. The 45ft. turntable was barely long enough to turn the later 4-4-0s and in 1889 a new 50ft. one was installed both here and at Keith which with 'safety and facility would deal with the latest engines'. The shed deteriorated badly over the years; the steep roof helped to avoid snow accumulation but timber frame buildings, moving quietly even under the gentle seasonal variations of sun and rain, could not long endure the Highland gales. So were many buildings

replaced in stone but at Helmsdale, when it was finally declared a ruin in the spring of 1899, the wooden frame and cladding was simply taken down and reassembled, with as little new material as the company could get away with. The whole lot blew down in a severe storm in February 1921, after years of creaking alarm and it was reconstructed yet again, this time to an odd unattractive form with low curved roof, reminiscent of those on certain Irish narrow gauge lines.

For many years the first up passenger train from the north to Inverness started from Helmsdale with a return working in the afternoon or early evening and there was also a freight to Inverness, the men lodging there and returning the next day with the same engine. Thus three engines were required, in 1919 4-4-0 No.95 *Strathcarron* and two Barney 0-6-0s, Nos. 134 and 135. Things changed little over the years although different engines were drafted in from time to time. In 1929 a

Helmsdale on 11th June 1936, with *Ben Dearg*, 0-6-0 No. 17700 and class 5 No. 5015. Until the 1950s Helmsdale was both terminating and starting point for a number of Inverness trains; it also had to provide any pilot assistance that might be required, either north or south bound. Eight hour working meant that for many years past it was convenient to change crews there; moreover it provided a base for a snowplough, and a spare engine in the event of failure. *Photo: W. A. Camwell*

Big Ben No. 14420 *Ben a'Chait* was often there and later a 4-6-0 No. 14689 *Cluny Castle*. When the class 5s came north in 1935-36 Helmsdale continued to stable whatever Inverness sent up and used them on their workings as before although these were latterly change-over rather than lodging turns. A Small Ben was kept at Helmsdale for some desultory shunting and for assistance to County March summit or, more rarely, to Lairg, while an 0-6-0 was also usually present, for ballast trains and for snow plough work in winter. In 1947 these were No. 14409 *Ben Alisky* and Caledonian 3F No. 17587. After the Ben was withdrawn a Pickersgill 4-4-0 replaced it, regularly No. 54495. Helmsdale had a 55 ft. turntable by 1916 probably an extension of the old one, but in 1948 this was replaced by an articulated tractor fitted 'table of 60 ft., built by Cowans Sheldon.

After nationalisation and the rearrangement of shed codes Helmsdale was for the first time given an individual number, 60C, rather than being indicated as a sub shed of Inverness, while Dornoch and Tain became in turn sub sheds. The Dornoch branch was now being worked by the only two remaining Highland 0-4-4Ts, Nos. 55051 and 55053, one of which could generally be found resting at Helmsdale. After some difficult times they could be kept going no longer and a pair of Western Region 0-6-0 pannier tanks arrived in their stead.(see Dornoch, p35) . The branch was closed in June 1960 by which time steam working had almost ceased

on the main line. All passenger and goods trains now ran through between Inverness and Wick and the shed had become redundant. One or two diesels seem to have stabled there on occasions until some time in 1961, and with their last departure the shed can be deemed to have finally 'closed'.

The second roof at Helmsdale. Ruined by 1899, the shed was renewed in a fashion reminiscent of the much more enduring building at Dingwall. *Photo: Bernard Matthews collection.*

14410 *Ben Dearg* on 11th June 1936. From *Strathcarron* and two 0-6-0s in 1919 (see text) the complement had declined to two engines only by 1935, No. 14403 *Ben Attow* and Barney 0-6-0 No. 17703. A visit in the summer of 1937 was recorded in *The Railway Observer*: 'At this small depot only two Highland engines were in evidence No. 14405 *Ben Rinnes* and a Barney, 17700'. *Photo: W.A. Camwell.*

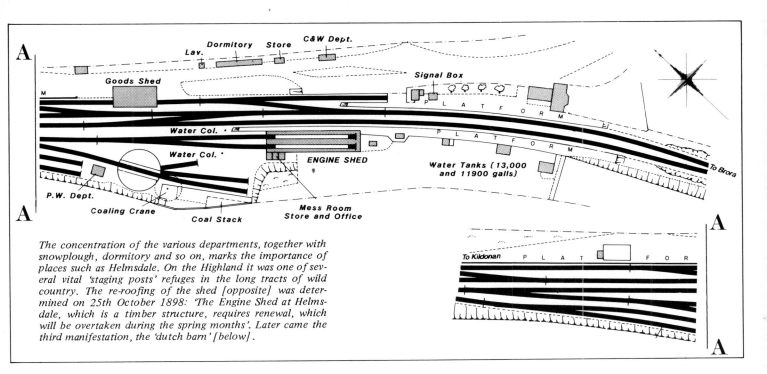

A
Lav.
Dormitory Store C&W Dept.
Goods Shed
Signal Box
M
P L A T F O R M
Water Col.
P L A T F O R M
Water Col.
ENGINE SHED
To Brora
P.W. Dept.
Water Tanks (13,000 and 11900 galls)
Coaling Crane
Coal Stack
Mess Room Store and Office
A
A

The concentration of the various departments, together with snowplough, dormitory and so on, marks the importance of places such as Helmsdale. On the Highland it was one of several vital 'staging posts' refuges in the long tracts of wild country. The re-roofing of the shed [opposite] was determined on 25th October 1898: 'The Engine Shed at Helmsdale, which is a timber structure, requires renewal, which will be overtaken during the spring months'. Later came the third manifestation, the 'dutch barn' [below].

To Kildonan
P L A T F O R
A
A

Helmsdale on 15th June 1949, with *Ben Alisky*. The Ben still has its LMS Northern Division shedplate, high up on the smokebox door. *Photo:- H. C. Casserley*

Helmsdale in August 1955, the line curving up into Strath Ullie. For three years the limit of the North line, it served first as operating terminus and thereafter as convenient and useful 'break' in the workings northwards. The great loops taken by the Highland main line as it approached Caithness to terminate at Wick and Thurso mean long and exacting locomotive work - around halfway a locomotive and p.w. retreat would prove most prudent, and this was the role determined for Helmsdale. *Photo: J.L. Stevenson.*

Engines for the Dornoch branch were dealt with at Helmsdale; various ancient types survived about the country as the 1950s drew to a close, through the special nature of the lines upon which they worked. The Wenford Bridge branch with its 2-4-0Ts in Cornwall (there are others) would be a good companion separated in distance from Helmsdale and Dornoch almost as far as it is possible to be in Britain, but joined by years of operating tradition. *Photo: W.A. Camwell*.

The Great Western and Western Region formed an attachment to the 0-6-0 tank locomotive, beyond what proved to be the strict demands of traffic (this manifested itself again in the 1960s orders for D95XX 650 hp 0-6-0s) and orders in 1947 for 94XX engines and later, 16XX, proved over optimistic. There were various efforts made to disperse some of the engines about the British Railways system but the Dornoch branch was just about the only one to meet with success. *Photo: W.A. Camwell*.

Helmsdale on 21st June 1960. It was entirely in the traditions of Scottish locomotive work that the outlandish pannier tanks should be so readily accepted, yet a paradox that duties so well suited to the class should be found so far from home.   *Photo:- W.A.Camwell*

Pannier tank No. 1646 alongside 5MT 4-6-0 No. 44718, a juxtaposition familiar only in certain parts of the country - oddly in the south, in Oxfordshire and in the north west at places such as Birkenhead and Shrewsbury. The tanks were redundant in 1960 with closure of the branch and the shed was effectively closed about that time, or the following year. They found their way south to Perth, lying at the rear of the shed until called for scrap. *Photo: N.E. Preedy.*

61

Inside the great roundhouse at Inverness, around 1913. It was 'the very heart' of Highland locomotive running, a quality only enhanced by its 'closed-in' *inner sanctum* features.
Photo:- John Hooper collection

Inverness

On 6th November 1855 the Inverness & Nairn Railway opened their fifteen miles of line with two 2-2-2s, *Raigmore* and *Aldourie*, joined within a couple of years by *St. Martins* and *Ardross* while construction was pressed on eastwards by the Inverness and Aberdeen Junction Railway towards Keith, reached in August 1858. Soon a start was to be made on the long struggle north into Caithness and south to Perth, from Forres via Dunkeld.

For the opening of the Inverness & Nairn an engine shed was established on the north side of the line, as it entered Inverness station; while beside it Lochgorm Works soon began to take shape within a triangle, bounded by the north and east platforms and the connecting Rose Street curve. Little is known of this shed but it occupied that part of the Works buildings nearest the east line platforms. (The Parliamentary plan shows a rectangular building, matching the subsequent Works layout). It lay close by the Nairn line and in May 1856 an unfortunate error by a pointsman led to the diversion of an arriving train into the shed. It was doubtless a novel experience for the passengers but the hapless pointsman lost his job.

In 1862 there were sixteen engines in operation and a considerable increase in prospect upon connection with the south, destined for the following year. Land for a fine new shed was available on the south side of the line bordering Eastgate and Millburn Road, an area originally, it is recorded, 'lying under water'.

A Minute of 4th October 1862 records the decision to establish a new engine shed: 'Resolved . . . . . to instruct the Engineer to prepare plan of a new Running Shed at Inverness. . . . . capable of housing twenty Locomotives. . . . .in preparation for opening of Inverness & Perth line . . . . .next summer'. On 17th February 1863 Tenders for 'Running Shed & Workshops at Inverness' were considered and approved: 'John Hendrie, Inverness . .Mason, Carpenter, Plumbing & Glazier work . £4,952. Butler & Co. Leeds . . . . Iron Roof, £1,144 14/- 5d Ormerod & Co. Manchester. . . . .Turntable, £320 . . . . .' Construction proceeded rapidly and the shed must have come into use later in the year. The Board was informed that in August 'four fifths' of the work had been paid for and Joseph Mitchell, the Civil Engineer, reported to the shareholders in January 1864 that 'the new shed . . . . had been brought into use . . . . during the past half year'.

HR No. 62 *Ault Wharrie* around 1905; among those beyond are *Huntingtower, Stemster* and *Perthshire*. It is next to impossible, now to trace the design origins of the Inverness roundhouse. Little enough in any company archive will betray much of the reasoning or thought behind any action, especially in the earlier periods, and the Highland records boast a brevity that at times descends to the taciturn. *Photo:- H. C. Casserley*

14675 *Taymouth Castle* at Inverness. From humble beginnings as 'a rectangular building now occupied by the Lochgorm works' (though its precise dimensions and location are lost to us) the Inverness roundhouse arose as a startlingly new building. Even with its original 21 arches it was wholly unlike any building then under construction in the North if not the whole of Scotland, unless it be the open roundhouse at Aberdeen, Kittybrewster. *Photo:- T.Middlemass*

Whether the Aberdeen and Inverness roundhouses were ever linked by common architect / designer or indeed any connection existed at all, however tenuous, remains an idle if fascinating notion. Certainly Inverness by a great margin was the best of the Highland sheds and the only other of comparable size, the straight shed at Perth, was dull by comparison. May 1930. *Photo:- H.C.Casserley*

Jones Goods No. 17919 in 1931. The sweep of the roundhouse, enclosing both the 'table and a considerable length of rail off it, effectively confined much of the work of the shed within a small space, a scene of almost unending turning, shunting and preparation. *The Railway Observer of* **August 1937 :** *Inverness - The roundhouse here was a scene of great activity, and most classes represented, including 'Lochs', 'Bens', 'Castles', 'Barneys', and two more of the four 'Jones Goods', 17926 and 17917. The shed foreman could remember as far back as the time of the 2-4-0s, and recollected going to Perth to take delivery of 'Loch Laggan', then new in 1896. Warming to his subject, he talked eloquently of the 'good old days' of clean engines, and when each man had his own mount. To quote the foremans picturesque description, 'if the driver was badly, the engine was badly as well.'* Photo:- Gordon Coltas

Impromptu tender, attached to one of the Dawsholm((ex-CR) tanks, from the Yoker sub shed (see Volume 5). No 16011 would presumably have been on the Inverness Harbour/Canal Basin branches, work which led to all manner of peculiar engines, peculiarly equipped, over the years. *May 1933: Several engines of the 4-6-0 Castle class are stored at Inverness, where the Harbour branch is now worked by 0-4-2T 15001, which has supplanted on this duty the little Stroudley tank No. 16119, now withdrawn.* Photo:- W. A. Camwell

Arrival of the Class 5 4-6-0s pressed the long-standing problem of clearances at Inverness ever harder; the Locomotive Committee were aware of the problem, at least as early as 1920 but the old arches remained an operating hazard until swept away in the late 1940s.   *Photo:- Photographer unknown*

The roundhouse about 1950. The 4-6-0s had begun to transform the place in the mid-1930s - seven were on the complement by 1935, and many more were beginning to work through from Perth. The process was well advanced by nationalisation. *Photo:- P.W.Melvill*

15010, an ancient Jones tank not long for this world, on 18th July 1931. Change was beginning at Inverness in this period, the first stirrings from far off to trouble this Highland fastness. Crab 2-6-0s had turned up to general astonishment, though their massive dimensions met with approval and 4F 0-6-0s Nos. 4312 to 4318 had spent a short stay. No. 15010 had been on station pilot duties about this time; the last of the 4-4-0Ts it was withdrawn in 1932. *Photo:- H.C.Casserley*

67

An Engineer's Report of 18th March 1864 relates: 'The New Locomotive Sheds at Inverness Station, capable of holding twenty-four Engines, have been completed and fully meet our requirements'. By the end of that year the locomotive stock totalled 55, although three of these certainly were 'in pieces'. The shed at first occupied a perfect semi-circle, set off by an ornate water tower of dressed stone. It was an imposing sight, marred only by a crudely mismatched 'Coal Bank', a low and broad stone platform to one side. 'A Fountain' was placed on the raised earth approach to the bank where at first only a small 'iron shelter' stood, housing a weighing machine for coal. It was not long before a substantial wooden stage in classic Scottish fashion was erected, a 'Coal Bench' proper.

The 45,000 gallon water tank, the great 'Marble Arch', stood apart for years, to become the most admired feature of the shed, something after the fashion of the Doric Arch at Euston. It is often said that the Arch was designed as part of a wholly circular roundhouse. This may not have been strictly true; the great portal (its tank to be 'of sufficient capacity to meet future needs') was designed quite evidently as a separate structure, dressed stone on all sides and was to serve as an entranceway, however extended the circle of the shed might become. It is understood that on plans submitted by the Inverness & Perth Junction line, when the Highland Railway itself was to come into existence, the roundhouse is shown as a full circle but with portions coloured differently, to indicate future intentions as to enlargement. The original semi-circle held twenty-one roads and in the event only ten further roads were added, five at either end. This is believed to have taken place in 1875 when 'improvements' were noted though it is difficult to be precise: the Highland records are economical to a fault in their wording; the term is employed to describe almost anything it would seem and it might refer to a new hydrant as much as a reconstruction of a shed. There was little room for manoeuvre around the closely-invested turntable and yard accidents were not uncommon. The doors suffered inevitable damage - Jones fined a fitter, Jas. Beaton, 2/6d on 17th October 1881 . . . 'for breaking a door of the steam shed by allowing an Engine to go against it'.

All tracks entered the shed through arches and what remained of the doors was taken off during or shortly after the First World War. The arches remained a hazard to staff especially on the arrival of the Cumming 4-6-0s and LMS standard types, which were a close fit. Consideration was given to widening the openings, to twelve feet, by the substitution of steel girders for the old stone uprights but the Locomotive Committee, meeting in October 1920 was not prepared to sanction the necessary expenditure, estimated at £1,500. It was not until about 1949 that the arches were taken away and light steelwork put in their place. The change rendered the shed interior subject to increased draught but smoke was borne away more readily. No part seems to have been put aside specifically for maintenance but engines out of steam were generally to be found on the ten 'new' roads between the original and later gables. A set of shearlegs

was the only large piece of equipment, standing astride a short length of track protruding through the shed wall at the south west corner. Lochgorm Works were always at hand for any work of a more onerous nature.

The turntable had been enlarged from the original 45 ft. to 55 ft. 2 ins. by 1901 and was replaced by a new one from Cowans Sheldon in 1914 at an odd length of 63 ft. 2 ins, dictated by the track geometry. Various incidents appear to have taken place, engines fouling the 'table or pit and the Chief Engineer, Newlands, was instructed to 'go into the question of an automatic block or any other such means of preventing such accidents in future'. Nothing seems to have resulted from his deliberations. The 'Coal Bank' was a primitive affair, low and backing onto Millburn Road. It could not be hoped that it might serve for long and a new wooden shelter was raised up in 1899:

'4th April 1899. Permanent Way Committee. Recommend . . . .

1. Laying floor of Coal Stage, Inverness, Loco Dept. with cast iron plates, £100

Big Goods, No. 17928 passing through The Marble Arch from the coal stage to the roundhouse in June 1927. *Photo:- H.C.Casserley*

2. Engine Pit on north access line of rails to the Inverness Turntable, including slueing of a siding and the removal of Old Engine Weighbridge thereon, £65.

3. Extension with timber of the present one Engine Coaling Stage at Inverness including roofing over present Stage and line on each side thereof, £300.'
This latter point raised some Highland eyebrows and an outlay of £190 only was agreed on 31st October 1899. The Highland was ever concerned with costs or rather the avoidance thereof and on 8th December faced with a requirement for Dormitory arrangements at Inverness, the Company . . . . 'decided as a temporary measure to fit up 2 old carriages, the cost of building being at present . . . . . prohibitive'.

The new stage employed some seventeen men and was replaced in its turn in 1935 by a mechanical coaling plant, together with ash disposal apparatus, to a pattern established as standard on the LMS (see *LMS Engine Sheds, passim*, in particular Volume One). A proper dormitory was put up much later, on a site close by the station. The shed invariably contained examples of most of the Highland engine types, and indeed in the

14395 *Loch Garve* by the old coal stage in 1931. This dated from 1899/1900 and though simple enough, replaced an even cruder 'bank' from which Inverness engines were coaled by hand for decades. *Photo:- Gordon Coltas*

Loch Ruthven in 1928. Inverness engines at this time were certainly well kept, something *The Railway Observer* could comment on in 1937 following the foremans remarks (p . 65): *It should certainly be added, though, that Inverness locomotives are cleaner now than most others of the present day, and no less than thirteen men and boys were observed polishing 'Ballindalloch Castle'. Whether this is exceptional or not is difficult to say. The Stanier 4-6-0 'six-footers', are of course ubiquitous by now, the only line on which they do not work being the Skye line, from Dingwall to Kyle of Lochalsh. Standard 0-6-0 shunting tanks are also to be found here and there, but the interest of the old Highland types has not yet vanished.* *Photo:- H.C.Casserley*

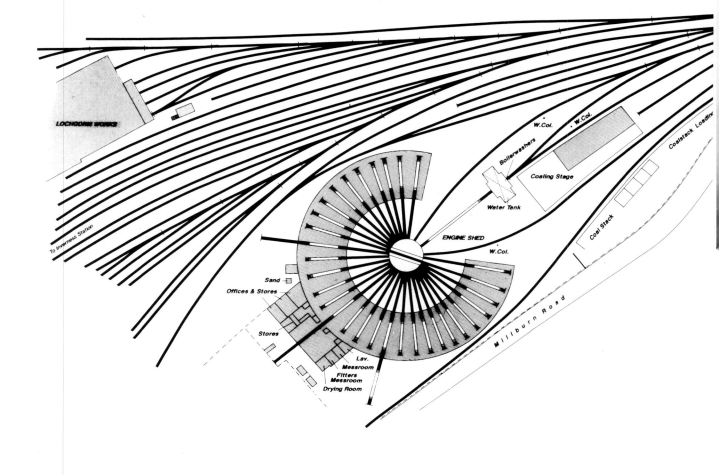

Labels within diagram: LOCHGORM WORKS; To Inverness Station; W.Col.; W.Col.; Boilerwashers; Coaling Stage; Coalstack Loading; Water Tank; ENGINE SHED; W.Col.; Coal Stack; Millburn Road; Sand; Offices & Stores; Stores; Lav.; Messroom; Fitters Messroom; Drying Room

Inverness roundhouse in its familiar Highland guise, before the LMS coaling plant arose to eclipse the 'Marble Arch'. Most repairs seem to have carried on in the works across the main line and the shed was accordingly ill-equipped in this regard; one factor in its omission as a 'concentration' shed in 1935. 'For policy and other reasons carriage wagon and local repairs at Lochgorm Works could continue', it was decided by the Board on 27th November 1924 [the same meeting ordered the closure or run-down of Perth, Kilmarnock, Barrow and Stoke works]. From February 1929 Lochgorm, it was ordered, should concentrate on 'light and service repairs only'. Kilmarnock was reprieved, to carry out work of a similar nature and all heavy repairs for the Northern Division were concentrated at St Rollox. Savings were estimated at £23,000 per annum, 'making the practical completion of the reorganisation of the Locomotive and C&W departments in Scotland'.

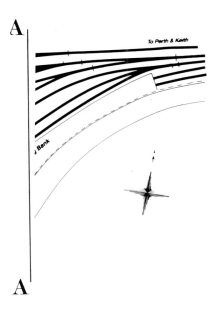

To Perth & Keith

Bank

A
A

Inside Lochgorm Works on 11th June 1936. The place was reprieved (as we have seen, left), as much in belated recognition of Scottish sensitivities as for any strictly operational purposes. *Photo:- W.A.Camwell*

The new coaling plant allowed the services of the team of coalmen to be 'dispensed with'. The LMS had been tardy in its use of the new mechanical aids to coaling and by 1933 was well behind developments elsewhere, principally on the LNER but also on the Southern Railway. It was to bound ahead before 1939 with a prodigious programme of investment and equipment amounting to a near revolution. *Photo:- Photographer unknown*

The coaler belonged to the smaller of two broadly standard types introduced from 1933/4. The Inverness example corresponded to the smaller 'No. 2' design, with a nominal capacity of up to 150 tons. *Photo Authors collection*

1914-1918 War a fair selection from other companies, on loan. In 1919 65 engines were allocated to Inverness, of a total stock of 165, the only shed to bear comparison being Perth, with 32. In 1935 the respective numbers were 47 and 32, though it is always difficult to know which outstationed locomotives are included, or excluded, from such figures. The Highland had a locomotive stock of 173 at Grouping but only 150 of these were taken into LMS ownership; otherwise changes during the first five years were few. One interesting arrival nonetheless was a Glasgow & South Western 0-4-0ST of 1881 which came to Inverness still in its original livery as No. 659 for work on the Harbour and Canal Basin branches. It later became LMS No. 16040 and remained at Inverness until withdrawn in 1932; other ex-G & SW arrivals included 0-4-4Ts Nos. 16081, 16083 and 16084, employed on sundry branch work for variously brief periods. Loadings on the Perth line became of increasing concern and led to the arrival of the six River 4-6-0s in 1928, originally built for the Highland and rejected, as has been related many times before. These engines were followed in 1929 by ten Hughes moguls, allocated to Perth but daily visitors to Inverness. They were well received ('a great success') but less welcome were seven 4F 0-6-0s, Nos. 4312-4318. Standard 3F tanks, Nos. 16416 and 16624 replaced the Highland tanks of 1903-4.

The first great change in the Inverness complement took place in 1935; after the arrival of class 5 4-6-0 No. 5023 at Perth in mid-August the previous

4-6-0 No. 5158 *Glasgow Yeomanry*, at Inverness in the 1930s. With the coming of the new 4-6-0s from 1935, serviced amongst standard coaling and ash lifting plants (the coaler rivalled The Marble Arch as local landmark) Inverness began to look a little like the LMS the length of the country, which was of course part of the point of the whole modernisation process. The allocation for June 1935 is of particular interest : 5P5F 4-6-0 : 5010, 5011, 5013, 5016, 5017, 5028, 5029; Loch 4-4-0 : 14381, 14386, 14394, 14395; Small Ben 4-4-0 : 14399, 14404, 14409, 14411, 14412; Castle 4-6-0 : 14675, 14676, 14681, 14682, 14685, 14689; Barney 0-6-0 : 17693, 17697, 17698, 17699, 17700, 17701, 17002; Jones 4-6-0 : 17917, 17923, 17927; Cumming 4-6-0 : 17593, 17954, 17955, 17956; CR 0-4-2ST : 15001; CR 0-4-4T : 15103; LMS 3F 0-6-0T: 16416, 16624. *Photo:- H.N.James*

year the new Stanier engines became available in great quantity, such that by June 1935 Nos. 5010, 5011, 5013, 5016, 5017, 5026 and 5029 were all at Inverness. Their ranks were increased to thirteen within six months, and the class was soon working to Wick. The class 5s became almost wholly dominant on the Highland line, illustrated in the 1942 allocation:

15th June 1942.

Class 5 4-6-0
5005, 5006, 5007, 5008, 5009, 5010, 5011, 5012, 5013, 5014, 5015, 5016, 5017, 5018, 5053, 5066, 5083, 5084, 5090, 5098, 5120, 5121, 5122, 5123, 5124, 5159, 5160, 5161, 5162, 5192, 5319, 5320, 5359, 5360, 5361.

HR Clan 4-6-0
14762 *Clan Campbell*, 14763 *Clan Fraser*, 14764 *Clan Munro*, 14765 *Clan Stewart*, 14766 *Clan Chattan*, 14767 *Clan Mackinnon*, 14768 *Clan Mackenzie*, 14769 *Clan Cameron*

HR Castle 4-6-0
14678 *Gordon Castle*, 14685 *Dunvegan Castle*, 14689 *Cluny Castle*

CR 2P 4-4-0
14331, 14340, 14348.

HR Small Ben 4-4-0
14397 *Ben-y-Gloe*, 14400 *Ben More*, 14401 *Ben Vrackie*, 14403 *Ben Attow*, 14404 *Ben Clebrig*, 14405 *Ben Rinnes*, 14408 *Ben Hope*, 14409 *Ben Alisky*, 14410 *Ben Dearg*, 14412 *Ben Avon*, 14415 *Ben Bhach Ard*, 14416 *Ben a'Bhuird* .

HR Loch 4-4-0
14392 *Loch Naver*

CR 2P 0-4-4T
15199, 15226.

CR 1P 0-4-4T
15103 (transferred from Stirling in 1934).

HR 0-4-4T
15051, 15053, 15054

CR 0-4-2ST
15001 (arrived in 1933).

SR D1 0-4-2T
2358, 2699 (on loan).

HR Superheated Goods 4-6-0
17950, 17951, 17952, 17953, 17954, 17955, 17956, 17957.

G & SWR 2-6-0
17821, 17822, 17829.

HR 0-6-0
17693, 17694, 17695, 17696, 17697, 17702, 17703

CR 2F 0-6-0
17330.

LMS 3F 0-6-0T
7333, 7541.

CR 3F 0-6-0T
16291, 16293, 16341.

CR 0-4-0ST
16011.

(Total 96 - includes outstations north and west of Inverness).

4-4-0 *Loch Ness* in June 1937. Locomotive coal was a principal traffic consideration; coal trains were a costly burden, for reasons of loading they were shorter than would otherwise be the case and were an operating nuisance. It was thus a considerable factor in the decision to dieselise. In this fashion the Highland lines could bear comparison with East Anglia and the West Country where coal, in the latter case, came often *by sea*.   *Photo:- H. C. Casserley*

The provision of coaling plants and other items was rigidly defined centrally, in keeping with the general policies pursued on the LMS by the 1930s. The reality was, however, an almost infinite detail variety at local level. The Inverness plant was built much after the fashion of the standard 'No. 2' unit, as noted previously, but this specification meant two bunkers, of 75 tons each, and at Inverness, as far as can be ascertained, only one bunker/jigger feed was in use. *Photo:- Brian Morrison*

The second bunker and jigger would have been visible in the photograph (top) of No. 57642 and a mirror image to that serving *Loch Ness*, (above). In effect, each plant was individually tendered for and built to whatever costs were sanctioned, with regard to local conditions. The best contemporary description of the Modernisation Programme is that of *The Railway Gazette* 1937. A fairly detailed account is given in volume 1 of *LMS Engine Sheds* (1981, and reprint 1987, Wild Swan) entitled 'A Quest for Efficiency'. A reappraisal of these years, together with the further developments (a largely unsung and late blossoming) into BR days appears in *BR Engine Sheds No.3 : London Midland 1920s to 1960s* by Hawkins, Hooper and Reeve, IRWELL PRESS. *Photo:- Tony Wright*

The roundhouse from above Millburn Road in April 1957. Only now, in its last years, had the transformation in engine power been all but made, all of it brought to nought by the astonishing pace of dieselisation. The first, ominously, penetrated to Inverness in this year. 5MT 4-6-0s had come to entirely dominate the principal traffics, with the last of the Highland locomotives leaving in 1952; goods 4-6-0 No. 57954 had gone in October of that year with the last Clan, 54767, *Clan MacKinnon,* going in January 1950. LMS 2P 4-4-0s had been tried in 1947, Nos. 566, 592, 605, 619 and 666 but were considered poor tools and soon returned south. More familiar CR 3P 4-4-0s then followed, displaced by new 2-6-4Ts in the Glasgow area and these, with ex - CR 0-6-0s inherited the various scattered sub sheds until the closures of the early 1960s.   *Photo:- J.L.Stevenson*

8F 2-8-0s were ever unusual in Scotland, and particularly so in the Highlands but a few spent short periods at work. 8322 was a Perth engine at this time (10th April 1946) and like others was fitted with a 'wee plough'. A fair number had accumulated at Perth during the war but as a policy of concentrating standard types all had gone to England by the end of the following year. Snow ploughs in Scotland of course were not a matter of any particular note; they were routinely put to use most winters, the 'big ploughs' powered by 0-6-0s and Class 5s, or combinations thereof. *Photo:- H.C.Casserley*

'Tankie' No. 56038 on 26th July 1953, its 60A plate stubbornly in place. *Photo:- Brian Morrison*

Freight activity in the Second World War was such to render existing loops and yards inadequate and a 'secret' report of 23rd November 1942 proposed a new yard outside Inverness, which would bring diesel shunters into the district: 'Proposed new yard at Allanfearn. . . . . if provided, shunter should be diesel, to avoid engine running light to Inverness for coal water and stores and also a similar loco for Inverness Goods Yard, which can be used for replacement purposes, if necessary'. Nothing, however, came of these proposals. The Highland engines were increasingly put out of use after 1944 and in their place a number of Caledonian 4-4-0s and 0-6-0s came to the north, to Inverness as well as to Aviemore, Forres, Helmsdale and Wick. Further class 5s arrived and by June 1950 the character of the allocation (it includes Dingwall, Fortrose and Kyle) had altered considerably:

Class 5 4-6-0
44783, 44784, 44785, 44788, 44789, 44798, 44799, 44991, 44992, 45012, 45053, 45066, 45090, 45098, 45120, 45122, 45123, 45124, 45136, 45138, 45160, 45179, 45192, 45319, 45320, 45360, 45361, 45453, 45476, 45477, 45478, 45479.

CR 3P 4-4-0
54439, 54445, 54463, 54470, 54471, 54472, 54484, 54487, 54491, 54496.

CR 2P 0-4-4T
55129, 55160, 55199.

CR 0-4-OST
56011, 56038

CR 3F 0-6-0T
56262, 56291, 56293, 56299, 56341.

CR 3F 0-6-0
57591, 57597, 57634, 57642

HR Superheated Goods 4-6-0
57950, 57951, 57954, 57955, 57956

NBR Y9 0-4-OST
68108

The North British tank was an unexpected arrival but had only a brief stay in the north. Otherwise there were relatively few further changes until the onset of dieselisation in 1959.

With repair work much reduced at Lochgorm (it officially ended operations as an engine works the week ending 4th July 1959) alterations were effected so that it could serve as a diesel depot. For a short time diesel shunters and a few main line Type 2s could be found in the steam shed but early in 1960 Lochgorm opened for diesel maintenance, and activity at the roundhouse declined sharply. The Kyle line appears to have continued with steam until June 1961 and some steam working from Perth carried on for a few months after that. Active steam was reportedly reduced to three engines by August 1961, 0-6-0PT No. 1646, 2-6-2T No. 40150 and Caledonian 0-6-0 No. 57587 though this account may in part at least be doubtful. In store were ex-CR 4-4-0s Nos. 54463, 54491, 54493, 0-4-4Ts Nos. 55216 and 55236, 0-6-0T No. 56305 and 0-6-0 No. 57585. The roundhouse and the Marble Arch were finally abandoned and demolished, the ground now occupied by an extension of the cattle market.

Given the code 29H in the Perth district in 1935, Inverness became 32A in 1940 and 60A under BR. It is interesting to note that codes were then given to Helmsdale and Wick so that the 'District' arrangement came to resemble closely the Highland listing of old.

The diesels at Inverness in August 1960. The diesels went to more appropriate and better equipped quarters fashioned from part of Lochgorm Works and *The Railway Magazine* recorded the end of the roundhouse in 1962 : *The old roundhouse at Inverness was cleared of steam locomotives early in August, 1962, and now lies derelict with only a few stored wagons under its roof. The last steam locomotives stored in it were sent to Perth; these included Pickersgill 4-4-0s Nos. 54466, 54482, and 54495, and 0-4-4 tank No. 55269, also the ex - Western Region 0-6-0 pannier tank engine No. 1646*
Photo:- Ken Fairey

Keith about 1930. Built as a four road shed almost, maybe, in proclamation of supremacy (or at least the hope of) over the nearby arch rival Great North of Scotland. One half was discreetly done away with after ten years or so when it became clear that traffic would not meet expectations, but that a new shed would be necessary at Blair Atholl. The dismantled half of Keith saw a

Keith

Until the turn of the century, an abiding hostility characterised the two small companies in the northern parts of Scotland. Apart from a direct rivalry for certain traffics, bitter feuds had punctuated the construction and routing of some of the original lines, specifically where they met in Moray and Banffshire. Two lines of what were to become the Highland and the Great North of Scotland met in the late 1850s at Keith; the Inverness and Aberdeen Junction Railway (incorporated into the Highland in 1865) came to Keith in August 1858 and by making an end-on connection with the Great North of Scotland main line from Aberdeen created a through route between Inverness and the south. Both companies erected engine sheds from the first, large stone structures with arched entrances. The Inverness and Aberdeen Junction evidently anticipated a need for large scale facilities and acquired an extensive piece of ground on the north side of their main line bounded by the River Isla. Here was located a 39 ft. 3 ins. turntable, a water tank and large shed with at first, it would appear, two identical sections some 100 feet long, designed each for two roads. These are indicated in the Ordnance Survey of 1869 but only one road is shown to enter the section of shed furthest from the main line. The other section at least was built as a through shed with arched entrances accommodating two tracks at the east end but, according to the map, with only one emerging at the west.

Such a large shed might eventually have proved necessary, if Keith had served as the only gateway from Inverness southward but in 1863 a through route opened from Forres over the Grampians to Perth. A shed opened at Forres, the junction of the east and south lines and the part played by Keith was soon confined to certain of the Inverness-Aberdeen traffic. Some of this furthermore was soon passing between the companies at Elgin, the Great North of Scotland opening its Craigellachie and Coast lines throughout in July 1863 and May 1886 respectively. It was realised early on that Keith shed could be reduced in size and at the Board Meeting in January 1868, considering the need to build a new engine shed at Blair Atholl, the Civil Engineer was 'instructed to take down one half of the shed at Keith and employ the materials at Blair Atholl so saving £576'. The remaining half of the shed proved quite adequate and in due course the arches at the west end were blocked up to make the building single ended. The dismantled section was then represented only by its single road, retained as a siding by the north wall, originally the partition wall. The original communicating arches remained visible to the end, but with the lower portions blocked up to create two windows. The 39 ft. 3 ins. turntable, adequate to turn only a 2-4-0 was still unchanged in 1887 but was then extended to 46 ft. 9 ins. In 1889 however it was replaced by one of 50 ft. 4 ins.

Keith on 28th May 1930. *Photo:- H.C.Casserley*

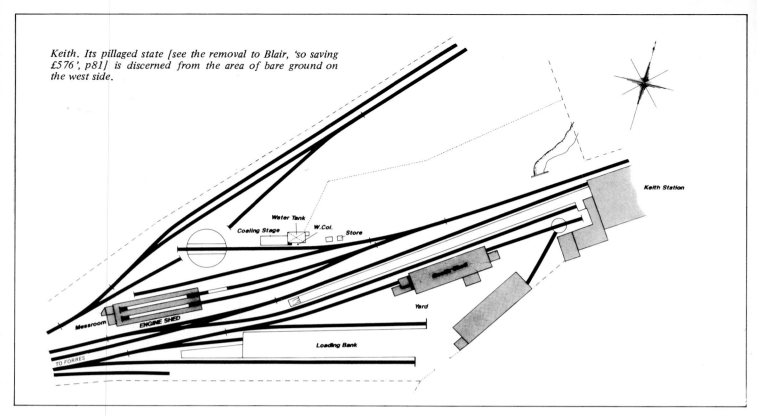

Keith. Its pillaged state [see the removal to Blair, 'so saving £576', p81] is discerned from the area of bare ground on the west side.

Keith Station

Coaling Stage
Water Tank
W.Col.
Store

Messroom
ENGINE SHED

TO FORRES

Loading Bank

Yard

17704 and 14400 at Keith on 25th September 1935. One of the numerous Inverness outstations, LMS organisation reduced them further to the simplest of sub sheds, often little more than standing ground for a locomotive. For much of the Highland period a single 4-4-0 sufficed as the 'allocation' though in the 1930s an 0-6-0 and a 4-4-0 seem to have become customary, as above. By November 1935 17704 was still there but 14400 *Ben More* (one of the several Bens we encounter again and again in this text) had been replaced by 14408 *Ben Hope*. *Photo:- W.A.Camwell*

Keith roofless and derelict on 11th September 1951, ex- CR 3P 4-4-0 No. 54482 passing on the 10.52 Forres - Keith train. The far wall originally divided the two parts of the shed and the windows are revealed to be bricked-up archways. *The Railway Observer* had noted in July : *The HR shed at Keith is now partly demolished having been disused for several years. The ex- LMS locos still use the turntable however and clean fires in what remains of the loco yard*

Photo:- John Edgington

'5th February 1889 . . . . .Replace present Engine turntables at Helmsdale and Keith . . . . . .with new ones of steel, of 50 ft. diameter for the purpose of turning with safety and facility, the longest Engines and Tenders in the Co's possession, at a cost for both Tables of £760'. This was still to prove too short a diameter for the later Highland Castle 4-6-0s and it was extended some time after 1920 to 55 ft.

Keith operated as an outpost of Forres and stabled only two or three engines, 2-4-0s in early days but from the Drummond era usually a Ben and a Barney 0-6-0. When the Highland opened their Buckie line in 1884 a shed was provided at Portessie (q.v.) but this was closed in November 1907 and Keith shed was thereafter responsible for the branch until its closure in August 1915, probably using a Yankee Tank, although a Small Ben is also known to have appeared.

The station at Keith, a rather make-shift affair, had only two through platforms, serving respectively the Highland line to Inverness and the GN of S Craigellachie services, the layout such that it was considered easier to change engines on Aberdeen to Inverness trains *before* entering the station, a cumbersome arrangement. This struck most visitors (and there were many, for the High-

land railways drew them, in numbers, despite the effort required to get there) as odd, that such a country station should adhere to such practices. It merited recording, as on 26th August 1937, when B12 4-6-0 No. 8536 on the 11.50 a.m. from Aberdeen was observed to draw to a halt east of the platform, for No. 14676 *Ballindalloch Castle* to take over for Inverness, and bring the train into the station. Through engine workings had been instituted between Aberdeen and Inverness in 1908 but were discontinued on the outbreak of war and not resumed until after Nationalisation, when at last the old company barriers were removed.

The Highland shed was abandoned soon after Nationalisation but the turntable and associated tracks remained in use probably until the end of steam in 1961. The building stood roofless with its tracks removed by the middle part of 1951 but the side walls were still standing as late as March 1961 and the siding behind the north wall held three stored engines, 2P 4-4-0s Nos. 40604 and 40618 together with 0-4-4T No. 55185. The GN of S shed, which underwent extensive reconstruction in 1954, latterly provided for any stabling accommodation that might be necessary for engines off the Highland section. This building is now in industrial use.

Kyle shed with Cumming 4-6-0 No. 17953, June 1936. The place was exquisitely neat, proudly maintained like many of these Highland sheds. A virtue was made of the old vehicle body accommodation, clean and ordered; elswhere such basic provision could easily sink into verminous neglect. Even the piles of clinker assumed an ordered look. *H.C.Casserley collection*

Kyle of Lochalsh

The shed at Kyle opened with the extension from Strome Ferry in 1897, its turntable and coal stage hewn from the living rock to the north of the station. The single track main line passed on one side and the sea, since reclaimed, lay upon the other. The new pier at Kyle was a bold development replacing the less convenient Strome Ferry for access to the Western Isles; there was a considerable traffic in fish, well to do visitors (and some less well off) came to gaze upon the Cuillins and there was a seasonal movement of Skye and Lewis natives, seeking work around Inverness.

Traffic on the Dingwall and Skye Railway after 1897 was largely given over to the little Skye Bogies, 4-4-0s built between 1882 and 1901. In 1919 Kyle had six of these but larger engines were by now appearing regularly, Straths and Small Bens. These gradually took over as the Skye Bogies were withdrawn between 1923 and 1930 but increasing loads demanded six coupled engines; the 4-6-0 superheated Goods of

1917-19 came in 1928 and took charge of the great part of the traffic for some eighteen years. Two or three of the Jones Big Goods 4-6-0s of 1894 were made available from 1933 and were equally successful on summer passenger trains; lacking steam heating apparatus they were hopefully not so employed in winter.

It is not clear how the Kyle allocation was arranged after Grouping - it seems likely that for most of the time it simply stabled engines out of Inverness and it is difficult to divine when an 'allocation' in the usual sense was present. On 1st July 1935 it was recorded as Jones Big Goods Nos. 17917, 17929 and 17930 'with 4-4-0 No. 14404 *Ben Clebrig* on loan for the summer season from Inverness'. Later that year, in November, the complement is given as two 4-6-0s, Nos. 17950 and 17951, and 14416, *Ben a' Bhuird*. The Ben at least was an abiding feature, provided every summer. It spent most days on a fairly light early morning train to Inverness, returning assisting a

17925 inside Kyle of Lochalsh on 19th June 1937, showing the economical Highland method of smoke removal. The neatness inside, more like a country church, matches the standards of the yard outside. *Photo:- H.C.Casserley*

17929 (and behind, 17956, 17957 and 17952) on 2nd July 1934 - Summer traffic taxed the little shed and a constant struggle was on to carry off the ash and clinker by wheelbarrow.   *Photo:- W.A.Camwell*

Immaculate Strath, No. 100 *Glenbruar* inside the shed. Despite severe gradients the Kyle line was worked for many years by such small locomotives, most notably the Skye Bogies with 5ft 3ins driving wheels. As late as 1919 the allocation at Kyle was six out of nine members of the class.
Photo:- J.L.Stevenson coll.

Jones Goods No. 17925 on 18th June 1937. The Skye Bogies had been withdrawn between 1922 and 1930 and from 1928 the Cumming 4-6-0s became increasingly associated with the line. The Jones Goods appeared in 1933 but had all been taken out of service by early 1940.   *Photo:- H. C. Casserley*

Kyle on 30th June 1938. Cumming 4-6-0s remained very much in evidence at the shed until 1946 when replacement of the turntable enabled regular working of the Stanier Class 5s. Small Bens provided additional power in the 1930s and on 8th June 1935 the complement amounted to four engines, Jones Goods No. 17929 with Cumming Goods Nos. 17950, 17952 and 17957. The following November recorded 17950 and 17951 and 14416 *Ben a 'Bhuird. Photo:- R.J.Buckley*

Kyle of Lochalsh, a remarkable Highland site: much of it can be traced today and the excavations required for the turntable and coal stage are likely to remain for several lifetimes, at least. The cutting through rock to achieve the desired site necessarily imposed restrictions on the layout and it could never be altered without a discouragingly heavy burden of cost. Merely enlarging the turntable in the 1940s meant a carefully planned campaign, re-ordering the entire working of the Kyle line.

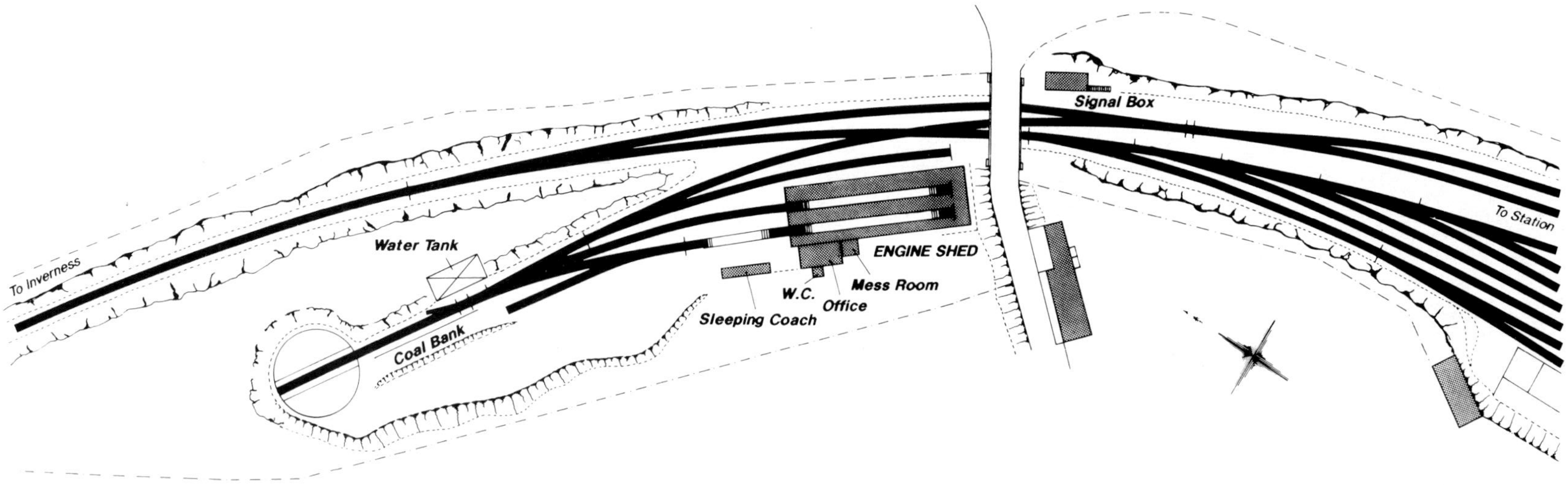

To Station

Signal Box

ENGINE SHED

Mess Room

W.C. Office

Sleeping Coach

Water Tank

Coal Bank

To Inverness

The coaling area and the turntable at Kyle were the strangest feature at the shed, hewn with great labour from the rock. The 21,000 gallon water tank rested on the rock face at its rear part, its excavation providing the blocks for its support wall at the front, and for the coal stage. Kyle shed was extremely restricted for space - the work of excavation had proved expensive enough in the first place and the Highland was disinclined to contemplate any enlargement. 22nd April 1952.

Photo:- H.C.Casserley

passenger train to Dingwall thence home with a freight. In August 1937 it was 14399 *Ben Vrackie*. In later years Caledonian 0-4-4T was also a regular resident; usually No. 55216, it was used for shunting the station and harbour lines.

During both World Wars the shed accommodated many strangers, especially during 1918 when there was a heavy traffic in naval mines between Kyle and Invergordon. From 1940 traffic was again heavy and Highland Clans began to appear on the line for the first time as well as more surprising oddities, including on occasions, it is believed, a G & SW R 2-6-0.

The 50 ft. turntable originally provided was too small for the class 5 4-6-0s; extension was difficult for the pit was closely bounded by rock but the LMS set about the further blasting necessary for enlargement to 54 ft. The reconstruction was accordingly protracted and services were worked by seven 2-6-4Ts, Nos. 2213-2216 and 2695-2697 lent to Inverness by Polmadie

during most of 1946. They worked the route most effectively, usually facing west and returning bunker-first. Once the new 'table was installed Class 5s began to work the passenger services but the Highland 4-6-0s were still to be seen on freight turns until their demise in 1952.

The Kyle line went fully over to diesel traction at the beginning of the summer timetable of 1961; the last steam working proper took place on 10th June and it was reported that '0-4-4T No. 55237 had been left at Kyle . . . . . . where three diesels stable overnight'. A Class 5, No. 44978 ran an RCTS/SLS tour to Kyle on 14th June 1962, when the turntable presumably was still available for use. Diesels appear to have used the shed for some time even after its partial destruction by fire but they are now stabled at the station. The shed retained its arched entrances until it was demolished but the turntable has been acquired by the Speyside Railway and installed in the pit at Aviemore.

The simple shelter seems to have been an LMS provision, and the pointwork alongside it demonstrates the cramped nature of the layout. This narrow, constrained 'alley' determined the entire sequence of operation - entry to the yard, turning and coaling and release to stable in the shed, or return to the station for the next working. *Photo:- H.C.Casserley*

45631 on 27th August 1952, an uneasy resident in a shed intended for minute 4-4-0s.   *Photo:-   John Edgington*

(Left) 'The class 5 'table', enlarged with such effort at the end of the Second World War, in use in 1954. There were very few turntables like this, with such closely invested sites; understandably, for installation costs were increased by bounds. Astride solid rock, the foundation work was less extensive than otherwise might be but paradoxically such sites, apparently sheltered, could prove difficult in high winds (Ilfracombe on the Southern is an almost exactly parallel case). Buffeting gales could strike with alarmingly unpredictable, if highly localised force within the restricted space, as the inert bulk of the locomotive moved through 180 degrees.

The last generation of coach body at Kyle, wartime 'Accommodation for Enginemen' put in during April 1942 at a cost of £1200.   *Photo:- A.E.Bennet*

The shed in August 1937 with **14406** *Ben Slioch* **and 4-6-0s Nos 17956 and 17957. The shed occupied (and the site still does) ground 'at the back of town', despite its closeness, a couple of hundred yards, from the station and the sea. The flat, wet area is now grassed over but on the sheds opening was more or less water logged, the 'High Water Mark of Spring Tides' running within yards of the turntable.** *Photo:- W.A.Camwell*

Leaving Kyle, the magnitude of excavation work was very apparent - the shed was used by diesel locomotives, for stabling purposes, in dogged pursuit of steam practice, even following destruction of much of the roof by fire. A Mr M. Watson wrote to *Model Railway Constructor* in April 1963; when there in September 1962 he had seen the shed 'without a roof. On further investigation I found that there had been a fire which had destroyed the roof completely'. The place was a puzzlingly tiny (this effect of *smallness* is always evident at shed sites) piece of ballasted ground but the blasted rockwork remains imperishable. *Photo:- G.H.Platt*

Tain on 11th June 1936. For years it was a peculiarly busy outpost - take *The Railway Observer*, reporting a visit on **9th July 1937** :some half dozen locomotives were noted in the morning. These were 14416 'Ben A Bhuird', 14409 'Ben Dearg', 14410 'Ben Alisky', 17693, 14386 'Loch Tummel', and one modern 'taper-boiler' passing through. 14390 'Loch Fannich', which had retained its red paint, used to be stationed here, but it seems that it disappeared towards the end of last year.   Photo:- W.A.Camwell.

Tain

The first shed at Tain opened in June 1864, when the railway arrived from Inverness, continuing some three miles beyond to Meikle Ferry and extended later in the year to Bonar Bridge. The shed was a lengthy timber structure 110ft. by 18ft. with a 17ft. 5in. turntable nearby; it enjoyed an eventful but prematurely terminated existence, serving originally as 'Temporary Engine Shed Accommodation' at Invergordon; the Highland found it hard to abandon even semi-derelict buildings and dismal piles of wood were periodically swopped about the system*. The move from Invergordon appears to have been less than successful for on 3rd February 1874 Tenders 'were received for the re-erection of the Engine Shed at Tain'. The Board resolved to accept one of £362 8/- 0d and were accordingly put out when the wretched building burnt down three years later:

Fire at Tain Engine Shed 20th April 1877
. . . caused by the carelessness of an Engine cleaner . . . .
Resolved: to make a claim on the Insurance Co. for
£400 being the value of the shed [!] and £295 for damage
to the Engines. Agreed . . to rebuild the shed in stone and
lime, and to dismiss the cleaner.

If the insurance claim was successful the wretched cleaner had probably done the company a favour - the new shed was in stone with the usual arched entrances, erected this time at the Inverness end of the station on the up side, while a 50 ft. turntable in the goods yard at the north end had by 1901 replaced the previous inadequate one. This was replaced in its turn in 1937, by a second hand 60 ft. Cowans Sheldon 'table dating from 1901. Refurbished and fitted with a vacuum tractor it was re-located behind the up platform and it thus became possible to turn a Class 5 at Tain.

The shed was concerned with local passenger and goods services to Inverness. Two Barney 0-6-0s only were shown allocated in 1919, while in 1935 there were three engines, No. 14930 *Loch Fannich,* which had been at Tain for a number of years, Barney 0-6-0 No. 17699

*Though this is, perhaps, a little harsh, The Company was very hard up and was equally prepared to transfer heaps of masonry about the Highlands.

Ex - G&SWR 2-6-0 No. 17822 fitted up for snow plough work with 14403 *Ben Attow* at Tain on 11th January 1942. It is not clear how an engine such as this would be received on the Highland; crews, in common with those on other Scottish lines took with apparent alacrity to most new types and only MR-derived 4-4-0s and 0-6-0s suffered anything approaching 'rejection' on the Highland. The G&SW mogul, it can be imagined, was very much a 'reject' even before it left for the north. *H. C. Casserley*

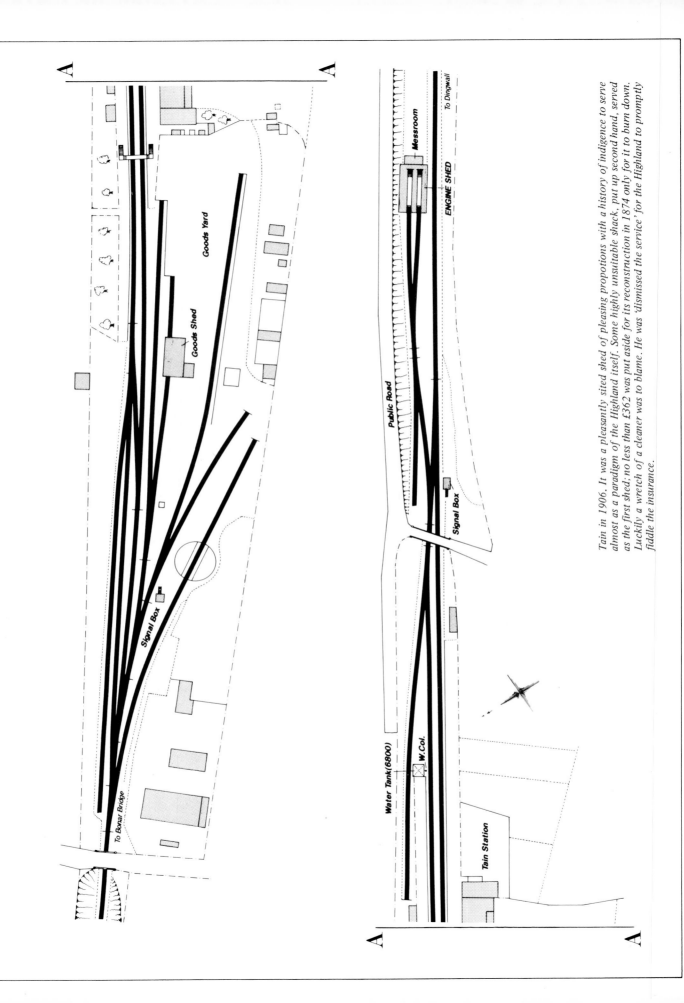

Tain in 1906. It was a pleasantly sited shed of pleasing propotions with a history of indigence to serve almost as a paradigm of the Highland itself. Some highly unsuitable shack, put up second hand, served as the first shed; no less than £362 was put aside for its reconstruction in 1874 only for it to burn down. Luckily a wretch of a cleaner was to blame. He was 'dismissed the service' for the Highland to promptly fiddle the insurance.

Goods Shed

Goods Yard

Signal Box

To Bonar Bridge

Water Tank (6800)

W.Col.

Public Road

Messroom

ENGINE SHED

To Dingwall

Signal Box

Tain Station

Ex - CR 4-4-0s at Tain on 20th June 1960. They came to be more or less ubiquitous in the last years of the Inverness 'sub - sheds' (though Tain was placed under Helmsdale by British Railways) and only succumbed at the last to diesel sets. 'Everyday life' at these Highland engine sheds is poorly recorded. The English branch engine shed had similar qualities of somnolence (classically, perhaps, on the Great Eastern) but only in Scotland it seems, could engines so often be stumbled upon, apparently unattended by the side of a field.   *Photo:- W. A. Camwell*

No. 54480 on 9th September 1953. What measures might have been taken to prevent fire during summer drought are unknown. There was presumably a risk with so many steam locomotives about but in the vastness of the hills it was presumably left to chance.   *Photo:- Brian Hilton*

and a Big Goods, No. 17930. During both World Wars the shed seems to have been heavily engaged servicing engines working to Invergordon with naval traffic. Photographs taken in 1942 show a Clan and a G&SW 2-6-0 amongst the engines stabled there.

For long regarded as an outstation of Inverness, Tain was after Nationalisation placed under Helmsdale, which became 60C. Two Caledonian Pickersgill 4-4-0s were at Tain by 1950, commonly Nos. 54470 and 54480, but their work here was finished when the Inverness-Tain local services were taken off in June 1960. This date almost certainly marks the closure of the shed. It continued in use for wagon storage for some time but was later demolished.

54480 again, in August 1949, preparing to work the 3.45pm local to Inverness. The longitudinal vents are presumed to have been a later, LMS, feature for the Highland would presumably have provided its usual individual pots. *Photo: J L Stevenson*

Further preparation at Tain, 22nd July 1959. The requirements for a shed such as this were exceedingly simple - coal could usually be topped up at Inverness - the plant there avoided the labour of hand shovelling - whilst firebox and smokebox debris could be carted off in a wagon every so often - assuming an obliging local could not find a use for it.
Photo:- P.Hutchinson

Tain on 30th June 1955. *Photo:- R.F.Roberts*

Tain in 1955, dozing amidst the sky and fields, in fashion unchanging over eighty years or more. *Photo:- T. J. Edgington*

Ben Rinnes at Thurso on 19th May 1928. The branch was worked by tender engines, most notably the Ben classes, for very many years, the trains generally running from Wick and back, through Georgemas Junction. This was the practice before the Second World War but it was only partly restored, for a short time, after 1945.   *Photo :- H.C.Casserley*

Thurso

The shed here opened with the line from Georgemas in 1874, a solid stone building to house the branch locomotive. The Manchester Railway Steel Plant Company provided a 45 ft. turntable (enlarged by 1920 to 52 ft., through 3 ft. 6 ins. extensions at each end) for tender engines working to Thurso. The line was to prove the principal mainland link with the Orkneys, mail and passengers travelling by van or bus from the terminus to Scrabster Harbour and 4-4-0s worked to Thurso almost until the 1960s.

In Highland and LMS days it was the custom to use tender engines on the branch though a Yankee Tank was also recorded, 2-4-0s followed by 4-4-0s of increasing size as they were displaced from elsewhere. No.130 *Loch Fannich* was there by 1915, aided as necessary by Ben classes. Castles visited on occasion but only 'filling in' from Wick, and they could not use the turntable. Clyde Bogie No.79 *Atholl* was at Thurso in 1919 and a Strath, No. 95 *Strathcarron* in 1923. Thereafter Small Bens characterised the work, commonly No. 14402 *Ben Armin* and No. 14405 *Ben Rinnes*. Bens continued prominently into the BR period and Nos. 54398 *Ben Alder*, 54399 *Ben Wyvis* and 54404 *Ben Clebrig* all appeared in their last years.

Freight working had been very heavy in both World Wars and even in 1949 enough remained* for an 0-6-0, No. 57585, to be still at Thurso, along with *Ben Clebrig*. Pickersgil 3P 4-4-0s worked the branch after this until a 2-6-2T, No. 40150 arrived, in May 1956. This appears to have stayed at Thurso** more or less until the end of steam. It was still there, reportedly, in January of 1961, though with dieselisation of the main line services more or less complete its removal was only months away. 40150 was still at Thurso in April but very soon after a Type 2 had taken over; 'Thurso . . . . . stables diesel overnight'. The locomotive now usually spends a week at a time at Thurso and stables at the station; the shed still exists, in some form of industrial use.

*In part at least, associated with construction of the Dounreay reactor.
**To what good effect is not clear - 4-4-0s should still have been around to relieve the 2-6-2T - it was apparently, 'not much use'.

14405 *Ben Rinnes* **continues it turn on 19th May 1928. During the summer months and in the fishing season Loch classes were frequent visitors and from the 1920s Castles were observed occasionally. They were only used from Wick on 'fill-in' turns and never used the Thurso turntable.** *Photo :- H.C.Casserley*

Thurso shed was unusual in retaining its turntable immediately outside. As we have seen this was a fairly primitive English practice which possessed maximum potential for inconvenience and accident. In England small sheds of this disposition were still being put up some years into the twentieth century. If there had been more money about a new larger 'table would probably have been put in alongside; as it was the Highland contented itself with bits of extension rail bolted on at each end.

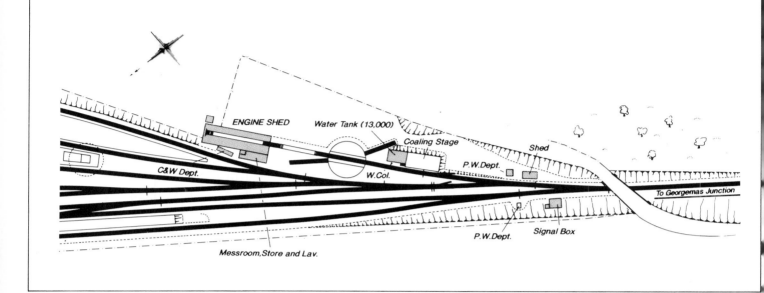

Newly renumbered Small Ben No 54404 *Ben Clebrigg* **in August 1949. The simple rail extensions, lengthening the 'table from 45ft to 52ft, would not have improved the working of the turntable.** *Photo:- J.L.Stevenson*

Thurso in August 1934 with 14415 *Ben Bhach Ard.*

Photo :- W.A.Camwell

The shed, massively built, was ever neat and tidy, and regularly whitewashed inside after Highland fashion. It could stand empty for much of the day, and when in use the engine was usually a 4-4-0. Barney 0-6-0s certainly turned up on goods when traffic was heavy; the Castles have already been noted but the only recorded visit of a Jones Goods seems to have been a railtour with preserved 103 in June 1962. *Photo :- Photographer unknown*

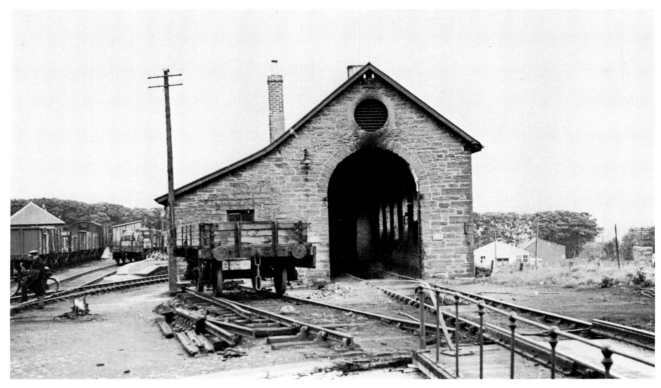

Thurso in August 1949.   *Photo :- J.L.Stevenson*

Thurso terminus. It had an all over roof, albeit of very short length, and it was Highland custom to avoid locomotive smoke at all costs. This made for a beautifully kept station (decorated in season with flower baskets) and the enjoyable spectacle of the train halting short while the engine detached, ran round and propelled it in.   *Photo :- Bernard Matthews collection*

Ex - CR 4-4-0 No. 54491 in September 1951. HR 54398 *Ben Alder* ended her days on the Thurso job, and CR 0-4-4T No. 55162 also worked on it in BR days. Freight had ever depended on 'special' traffic, coal and armaments for the fleet in both wars, and naval personnel and the atomic plant in the late fifties. The sheep sales, involving heavy movements of empty vehicles north from Inverness were features for years, with a shunting engine sent out from Wick. *Photo :- B. Hilton*

No. 40150 familiar at Thurso to the last but used often with reluctance, on 20th August 1957. It had arrived in May of the previous year. The branch diesel now stables in the station, though the sanctity of the overall roof was strictly observed, until a dark day in 1984, when exhaust fumes polluted the station, probably for the first time. *Photo :- A.R.Goult*

No. 26 *Braham Castle* at Wick. Castles and Jones Goods were familiar engines from the 1920s, sometimes piloted by Lochs, or the Ben classes when traffic was heavy.   *Photo:- W.A.Camwell*

Wick

The shed at Wick opened with the line in July 1874; a two road double-ended stone building, it stood in the goods yard on the south side of the station. The original 45 ft. turntable was in 1901 replaced by one of 55 ft., transferred from Daviot, and at the same time some additional sidings were laid in. 161¼ miles from Inverness, Wick had only a small allocation to assist main line working, to cover for failures and to provide spare engines for the Thurso and Lybster branches. In 1919 six were shown to be there, two Straths Nos. 89 *Sir George* and 91 *Strathspey;* Clyde Bogie No.83A *Monkland;* and old 2-4-0 No 37A used as snowplough engine in winter and perhaps the odd ballast train at other times; a little Lochgorm Tank No. 49A as shunting pilot or spare for Lybster; and oddest of all, the former Duke of Sutherland's engine, a 2-4-0T which became H.R. No. 118. It was as interesting a collection as one could wish to see at the end of the six hours (or more) trail north from Inverness. In 1935 Highland engines still predominated; two Castles, two Barney 0-6-0s and an 0-4-4T. Very soon afterwards the Class 5s commenced working on the North line but until the 1950s a Highland engine was invariably to be found at Wick. Of interest at this time was a Caledonian Drummond 0-4-4T, 15103, which was there for most of its last ten years, either working the Lybster branch or standing spare. Most remarkable of all was the arrival in 1941 of a Southern Class D1 0-4-2T No. 2358 on loan to the LMS. its purpose at Wick was far from clear as, officially anyway, it must have been too heavy for the Lybster Light Railway.

Getting coal to the remote Highland sheds was ever a problem - one factor indeed in the decision to diselise the North of Scotland first and it made sense to stack coal at Wick in some considerable quantity. It was loaded from an open platform in crude and time consuming fashion and it is some measure of locomotive activity at Wick during the last War that a small coaling plant of the elevated tub sort was erected. A unit of the 'Lynn' or 'Stranraer' type (after the first sites so blessed) came into use on 7th June 1943, at a cost of £6500.

0-6-0 No. 17703 at the rear of Wick shed, 19th May 1928. Wick remained a haunt of pre - Grouping types, sucessively downgraded from grander tasks. By 1935 14679 *Blair Castle* and 14692 *Darnaway Castle* were there, with an 0-6-0, Jones Goods No. 17926 and 17930, and two 0-4-4Ts for the Lybster branch, 15051 and 15054. *Photo:- H.C.Casserley*

Wick from the east about 1960. The shed had been re-roofed a short while before this, with a system of longitudinal venting; it was less crude than it might have been but the building suffered through the loss of its elegant Highland 'pots' (below). *Photo:- J.L.Stevenson coll.*

Jones Goods 4-6-0 No. 17930 with 14689 *Cluny Castle* **beyond and behind that, 14385** *Loch Tay* **and 0-4-4T No. 15051, on 11th. June 1936.** *Photo:- W.A.Camwell*

After nationalisation Wick received a code for the first time, 60D, with Thurso as its sub shed. The mid-1950 allocation consisted of the last three Small Bens Nos. 54398, 54399 and 54404, together with C.R. 4-4-0 No. 54445 and 3F 0-6-0 No. 57585. The Bens had all gone by the end of 1952 and further C.R. 4-4-0s had arrived as replacements, Nos. 54459, 54491 and 54496. Dieselisation came in 1960-1 but Wick still maintained a steam branch engine at Thurso, latterly 2-6-2T No. 40150 which was to be seen there as late as April 1961. The last steam engines at Wick were reported to have been 4-4-0 No. 54495 and Class 5s Nos. 44785 and 45117, the latter two retained whilst doubts about the abilities of the diesels to handle snow ploughs were resolved. It was decided that the 4-6-0s could indeed be sent away (the new 'big plough' was adapted from a locomotive tender) but it often needed three diesel locos and even then derailments were not unknown. The shed was used at first for diesel stabling but the locos were later moved to the station.

The 0-4-4T, 15050, on 21st. May 1928, the regular Lybster branch engine (it carried the name *Lybster* as No. 53/53A) for many years. It was withdrawn in 1929. *Photo:- H.C.Casserley*

The locomen at Wick are something of a race apart, spending much of their time pounding over the boundless wilderness up to the County March at Forsinard and eventually down Strath Ullie to the contrasting beauty of the shore between Helmsdale and Brora. Nowadays they seldom come south of Lairg but in earlier times the passenger men anyway would go through to lodge at Inverness. Caithness and Sutherland can look superb in summer but when the blizzards descend it can be a fearsome place and in the past, without benefit of radio communication, a failure or a blockage in mid-section must, in severe weather, have been a terrifying experience.

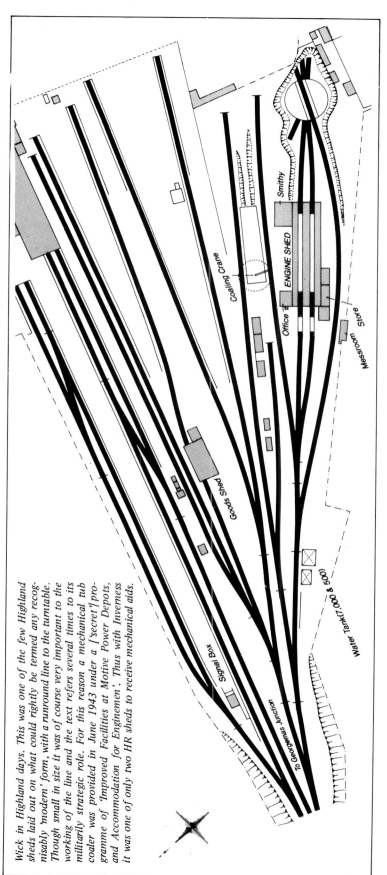

Wick in Highland days. This was one of the few Highland sheds laid out on what could rightly be termed any recognisably 'modern' form, with a runround line to the turntable. Though small in size it was of course very important to the working of the line and the text refers several times to its militarily strategic role. For this reason a mechanical tub coaler was provided in June 1943 under a ['secret'] programme of 'Improved Facilities at Motive Power Depots, and Accommodation for Enginemen'. Thus with Inverness it was one of only two HR sheds to receive mechanical aids.

Wick with original roof and one of the Lybster branch tanks (it had at one time been on the Killin line) on 26th. September 1935. The Lybster branch closed in 1944 and the small tanks were no longer required. *Photo:- W.A.Camwell*

The class 5 4-6-0s transformed workings on the Wick line, and elsewhere on the Highland. They powered the principal trains and a pair at least could frequently be found at the shed. Despite the 4-6-0s, many pre - grouping engines were still gathered at Wick; by 1950 the only three Bens to receive BR numbers were there, 54398 *Ben Alder*, 54399 *Ben Wyvis* and 54404 *Ben Clebrig*. Caledonian 4-4-0s and 0-6-0s followed : 1951 saw 54459 at Wick and 54491 in 1954, amongst others. 0-4-4T No. 55236 was a newcomer in the same year. *Photo:- H.C.Casserley*

108

By 1961 the shed stabled 'two diesels overnight' with 4-4-0 No. 54482 as spare. In October it was replaced by 54495, 'but in its turn it finished in December and worked back to Inverness.' The Type 2 diesels experienced difficulties with snow plough work and it is a tempting thought if the weather around 1960 had been persistently more severe a couple of steam locomotives for winter work might have been institutionalised at Wick and even elsewhere, carefully locked away in the summer months. But probably not. *Photo:- W.A.Camwell*

Wick yard in July 1957. With Inverness it was the only ex-Highland shed to be provided with mechanical aids, the tub hoist 'Stranraer' type coaler easing the turnround of class 5s to the south. The shed still stands today in private use. *Photo:-*

The **Highland** shed at Perth, the only establishment (apart from Inverness of course) that could begin to rival in size the many buildings to be found on other Scottish companies, the Caledonian, North British and even the Glasgow and South Western.   *Photo:- A R MacLeod*

SOME FURTHER SHEDS

BONAR BRIDGE

The railway reached here from Inverness in May 1863 and an engine shed with 'large turntable' were provided. These soon became redundant as the line was extended further north and the Highland board at their meeting in September 1867 agreed to sell both shed and turntable to the Sutherland Railway for 're-erection at Golspie'. Bonar Bridge remained the terminus for trains from Inverness until May 1871 when the next section from there to Helmsdale was brought into use throughout.

What happened to the shed and turntable thereafter can only be guessed at but one can be sure that the turntable at least saw use elsewhere. Conceivably, it was removed to Helmsdale and parts at least of the shed may have been similarly translated.

BURGHEAD

The line from Alves to Burghead opened at the end of 1862 and the terminus beside the pier was provided with an engine shed, tank and well. Built by the Inverness and Aberdeen Junction Railway, the Highland in October 1892 extended the branch two miles eastwards to Hopeman. This left the original terminus, engine shed and goods premises on a short spur and a new through station was constructed on the extension.

The original shed was burnt down (an evil fate pursued the earlier Highland sheds) in 1894 and replaced the following year by a substantial two-road structure in stone. Two engines were required from the 1890s when goods traffic in particular became quite heavy, mainly imported timber and agricultural products passing through the harbour.

The first regular branch engine had been a primitive 0-4-0 tank built in 1863 by Hawthorns of Leith for the Inverness and Aberdeen Junction and rebuilt in 1867 as an 0-4-2T, some other improvements being effected. Far from satisfactory in performance it nevertheless struggled on until 1879 when it was replaced by a Jones 2-4-0T No. 58, which remained at Burghead (rebuilt to a 4-4-0T in 1885) until 1892 when two Yankee Tanks Nos. 101 and 102, arrived and worked the branch during the period of its heaviest traffic. The passenger turn involved a daily mileage of around 100 and included one or two runs through to Elgin.

Two of the same class, Nos. 51A and 54, were still there in 1919, but in the last days of the passenger service - withdrawn in September 1931 - Standard LMS 0-6-0T No. 16415 was to be found and continued, latterly renumbered 7332, to reside in Burghead shed and deal with the goods workings. The shed is believed to have closed in 1938 and the branch thereafter was operated from Forres. It remains open for grain traffic today as far as Burghead. The shed albeit more or less intact in 1950 was wholly abandoned and was later demolished.

Burghead shed, probably in the 1930s and quite likely still open, though in the absence of the branch locomotive it would have been difficult to tell even then. Peering through the office window would probably been of little help and the Scottish habit of building two road sheds for the branches (comparitively rare in England) meant one road was frequently unused anyway, adding to the impression of general abandonment. *Photo:- W.H.Whitworth*

Standard tank No. 16415 at Burghead, probably around 1935. The first engine, as the text relates, had been a primitive 0-4-0T. It was delivered from Hawthorn Leslie in May 1863 'and was replaced on the Burghead branch by a more powerful engine in 1879, after which it was employed in Forres goods yard, shunting'. *Photo:- W.A.Camwell*

CARR BRIDGE

The first section of the Inverness-Aviemore Direct line, the 6¾ miles from Aviemore to Carr Bridge, was ready in July 1892 and a service of four trains daily was provided, based on Carr Bridge where a small wooden shed was built. Jones 4-4-0T No. 58 was sent from Burghead to inaugurate the operations and may well have have been the regular engine here until July 1897, when the completion of the next section of this massively engineered route enabled the service to be extended on to Daviot, 11 miles short of Inverness. The workings were still based upon Carr Bridge but a tender engine would probably now be required because of the greater mileage involved.

The Direct line was opened throughout between Inverness and Aviemore in November 1898; these short workings ended and Carr Bridge engine shed was put out of use and presumably afterwards dismantled.

DAVIOT

It is possible that an engine shed was established here for a short time as a base for construction work on the Inverness-Aviemore Direct line between 1890 and 1898. Certainly a 50ft. turntable was installed at Daviot in 1897-8, but removed in 1902 to Wick.

DUNKELD

In April 1856 the Perth and Dunkeld Railway opened a branch 8½ miles long, leaving the Perth - Aberdeen line of the Scottish Midland Junction Railway at Stanley, some miles north of Perth. The new line was worked at the start by the SMJR but this soon amalgamated with the Aberdeen company to form the Scottish North Eastern Railway, one of the eventual constituents of the Caledonian.

An old photograph dated c.1862 shows that a single road stone shed was provided at the south end of the station (which was built with an overall roof) on the down side. While this shed was never operated by the Highland, it was from Dunkeld that the main line was built north to Forres, opened throughout in 1863 by the Inverness and Perth Junction Railway which took over the Perth and Dunkeld in 1864. The I & PJR was one of the companies which came together to form the Highland in 1865.

The photograph shows that Dunkeld was the base for works trains involved in the building of the line northwards. The shed was still in existence in November 1877 when authority was given to remove it and extend the down platform at a cost of £1,064.

DUKE OF SUTHERLAND

The Third Duke of Sutherland played a leading part in the construction of the northernmost stretches of the Highland Line. In particular he financed the building of the 17 mile section from Golspie to Helmsdale while he shared with the Highland the provision of capital for the final section from Helmsdale to Wick and Thurso.

The purchase by the Duke of an engine for his own use - at first between Dunrobin and Helmsdale - required the construction of a shed. The engine was a 2-4-0 well tank delivered by Kitsons in 1870 and was kept at Brora, although no details of the nature of its accommodation seem to be known. Immediately on arrival it was used by the Duke to provide a public service between Dunrobin and West Helmsdale for seven months until the section was connected to the Highland line from Inverness. Thereafter it made many trips hauling a coach, also belonging to the Duke, mainly to convey guests between Inverness and Dunrobin but between 1881 and 1885 the engine worked a regular summer Saturday train for the use of the public from Golspie to Wick (or in certain cases to Thurso) and back. On all occasions the Working Timetable shows light engine workings from and to Brora. A small carriage shed was also built at Dunrobin (Private) station.

The Fourth Duke aquired a new engine in 1895, a neat 0-4-4T, (its predecessor was sold to the Highland) and it was decided to build a shed for it at Golspie, this being ready in 1896. The second *Dunrobin* was kept there and continued to haul the Dukes' coach, apart from

The Ducal shed at Golspie in October 1953, built in 1896 to accommodate the Dukes' second *Dunrobin*, the 0-4-4T. One coach would also normally be kept here, with a second in a shed at Dunrobin (see over). *Photo:- J.L.Stevenson*

absences during both World Wars, until the arrangement was quickly terminated by British Railways. In May 1950 after sale it departed to New Romney and subsequent emigration to Canada.

The shed was located in Golspie goods yard and was constructed in wood. It had a corrugated iron roof and had a small coaling bench at the entrance as well as a short turntable, presumably just sufficient to turn the 0-4-4T which had a wheelbase of 18 ft.1½inches. The shed appears to have been long enough to hold the engine and one of the Dukes' two coaches. Still intact in August 1955, it was later demolished.

Dunkeld about 1862. The station and engine shed are on the extreme left of the photograph. *Photo:- G.W.Wilson collection, ctsy Aberdeen University Library (EO567)*

Dunrobin shed, in June 1960, at the Duke's private station. Though the Ordnance Survey labels it 'Engine Shed' it served only as a carriage shed usually holding the smaller of the Duke's two coaches.   *Photo:- W.A.Camwell*

Fochabers (left), on 20th September 1935. It was unusual for the Highland to lurch into architectural extravagance but this is said to have been demanded by the Duke of Richmond Gordon who resided at the nearby Gordon Castle. *Photo:- W.A.Camwell*

FOCHABERS

The three mile branch from Orbliston Junction (formerly named Fochabers) to Fochabers Town was opened in October of 1893. Remote from Forres or Keith, the shed, in massively exuberant stonework, must have come into use at the same time; with arched entrance and high pitched roof it was probably just long enough to accommodate a four coupled tender engine.

The first occupant of the shed would very likely have been one of the Yankee 4-4-0 tanks but for some years from 1895 the 2-4-0T which the Highland bought from the Duke of Sutherland became the Fochabers branch engine appropriately named *Gordon Castle* and numbered 118. Later a Drummond 0-4-4T arrived here new, in 1905, No. 40 *Gordon Lennox* and was the regular engine until 1925, occasionally relieved by sister engine No. 45. However, in the later 1920s an elderly 4-4-0 was usually to be found, spending its declining years on what must have been an exceptionally easy duty, involving a daily mileage of only 42.

The latter-day engines at Focherbers included the last of the Skye Bogies, No. 14278 also a Strath, No. 14274 *Strathcarron*. Passenger services were withdrawn in September 1931 and the shed was closed, but goods traffic continued over the branch until March 1966.

FORT AUGUSTUS

The Invergarry and Fort Augustus Railway was completed in 1901 from its junction with the West Highland line at Spean Bridge. Passing through some fine scenery over its 24 miles and with heavy gradients, the railway lay out of use for the next two years while a legal wrangle took place between the North British and the Highland as to who should work it. The Highland was mindful of course that the line could be used by the NB as a stepping stone to Inverness. Eventually in June 1903 the Highland was awarded the dubious privilege of operation and lost no time in sending round two Yankee 4-4-0 tanks, Nos. 52 and 54, together with some coaches to commence services before the end of the summer. No. 54 soon returned to its home territory to be replaced by the almost new Skye Bogie No. 48.

The engineering features were constructed regardless of the meagre traffic prospects; the station at Fort Augustus had three platform faces and adjacent stood the handsome brick-built engine shed, of two roads. In April 1907 the Highland withdrew from the working having made a substantial financial loss but at least confident that the line would never be extended. Traffic was discontinued for the next couple of years but the North British then commenced operation and provided a Class

The extraordinarily lavish terminus of the Fort Augustus line, on 29th September 1935, rightly described by one the Reverend W.H.Nicholson as 'an unlikely venture'. Only one road of the shed was ever in use, with a turntable which could comfortably turn a North British Glen 4-4-0. The NBR worked the line after the Highland withdrawal with a 4-4-0T, then a 4-4-2T (see above) and in between with an 0-4-4T. After the Great War the 4-4-2T was in general use, working smokebox first towards Spean Bridge. When required an 0-6-0 (usually one of the 18½ ins. engines) worked goods, often on a mixed train. *Photo:- W.A.Camwell*

D51 4-4-0T and in later years usually a C15 4-4-2T. Passenger services ceased in December 1933 and the shed was finally closed, but an infrequent goods train was retained until January 1947. The shed was still intact in 1956.

KINGUSSIE

The Highland Railway Board at their meeting in March 1889 resolved to build an engine shed and 50ft. turntable at Kingussie at a cost of £1000.The shed, located behind the up platform at the south end, conveniently broke the long section of route between Blair Atholl and Forres, but a turntable had been provided from the start at Newtonmore and was much used by assisting engines working north from Blair Atholl and required to perform similar service on the way home.

The small wooden two-road structure appears to have housed only two engines, these in mid-1919 being No. 125 *Loch Tay* and a Clyde Bogie No. 81A *Colville*. One of the duties was a morning passenger train from New-tonmore to Inverness returning in the evening, these being generally known as 'The Johnstone Trains' after the driver who worked them for many years. The other engine was booked to give assistance southward, earlier working timetables showing the Kingussie pilot to assist the 10am and 4.0pm passenger train ex-Inverness to Dalwhinnie then the 7.5pm goods ex-Inverness to Blair Atholl and return assisting the 1.30am passenger train ex-Perth.

The Locomotive Committee at their meeting in August 1920 proposed to transfer the pilot working from Kingussie to Aviemore but the 'Johnstone Trains' apparently continued to be worked from Kingussie, as the 1923 Working Timetable shows their empty stock starting and finishing there. Moreover an LMS shed list dated August 1925 shows Kingussie still in business as an outstation of Aviemore. Two withdrawn Clyde Bogies are

believed to have been stored here in 1924, Nos. 76A *Bruce* and 81A *Colville*. No certain date is known for the closure of the shed but it probably had been effected by the end of 1926 with the transfer of the remaining work to Avie-more. The framework of the shed was still visible in 1936; the turntable is believed to have been taken out around this time but (and these things are by no means infallible) it still appeared on a System Diagram of May 1942.

KINLOSS

The Findhorn Railway was formed in 1859 to build a three mile branch from Kinloss on the Inver-ness and Aberdeen Junction Railway, 3¼ miles east of Forres to Findhorn, a small village with a harbour on the Moray Firth. An engine shed was provided at the junction its occupant a peculiarly hideous 0-4-0 box tank provided 'off the shelf' by Neilson & Co. Operations started in April 1860 but the line was soon in serious financial difficulties. It was acquired by the Inverness and Aberdeen Junction Railway in 1862 and passed to the Highland on its formation in 1865. No doubt a 2-4-0 would be provided on occasions when the tank was out of of action.

Traffic on the line continued to be very light and it was closed completely in January 1869. The station buildings at Findhorn are still very largely in existence and the course of the tracks can be traced on the pier, but of the junction station at Kinloss - some 300 yards east of the Highland station built subsequently - there is no trace although its location is roughly marked by a clump of trees.

An interesting point from Findhorn Railway days was that although the shed was at Kinloss the first train of the day commenced from Findhorn, not Kinloss. It is possible therefore that the engine ran 'light' carrying the mail in the morning, or worked an ECS.

Fort Augustus, one of the few British sheds seperated from its operators by miles of mountain and loch. It was put up by the lines promotors and was never 'owned' by either the High-land or the North British. *Photo:- W.A.Camwell*

Kingussie shed opened in 1889 primarily to have a pilot for working to Dulnaspidal, but was soon overshadowed by Aviemore, opened in 1898. It afterwards, served, apparenty, the recreational traffic; the area was a vast deer forest and sportsmen and women came in the season. *Photo:- W.A.Camwell*

INVERGORDON

Apart from the early 'Temporary Engine Shed Accommodation' noted under Tain (page 93) a later shed existed at Invergordon, associated with the working of the harbour. The matter is complicated by a variety of inconclusive Board and Committee Minutes and it is unclear whether the shed was ever considered part of the Running Department. It would appear to have been operated under the direction of the Harbour authority and later the Admiralty.

The matter first appears as early as March 1902 when the Locomotive Committee discussed the question of providing a '4-wheeled tank engine for Invergordon Harbour', and Drummond was empowered to purchase one, subject to satisfactory agreement with the Harbour Management. Nothing seems to have happened, but in April 1905 the Traffic and Works Committee recommended that a pug engine be provided for working Invergordon Harbour instead of horses. The following month Drummond reported that an engine had been sent but unfortunately added no details. In November 1909 the Way and Works Committee discussed the question of providing an engine shed with siding for the Invergordon Harbour branch.

During the 1914-18 war an enormous mileage of track and sidings were laid in at Invergordon, stretching south to Alness and operated for the most part by the Admiralty. There must have been heavy main line traffic associated with these installations . Despite the earlier reluctance to take any form of action some sort of shed must have been provided for the Estates Committee in September 1916 makes reference to a fire 'at the engine Shed Invergordon on 12th. August 1916'. Finally the Way and Works Committee in July 1918 affirmed that estimate should be obtained for 'a locomotive shed' at Invergordon. It must be concluded therefore that they were talking of a shed to replace an existing one, but with the end of the war, maybe, it was decided that no action was needed.

Invergordon has indeed long proved a puzzle; there is no mention in the Highland Working Timetables or similar contemporary material of arrangements for an Invergordon Harbour Co. engine to traverse HR metals so the assumption runs (i) there was no Harbour Co. loco, (ii) Harbour traffic was dealt with by an HR engine, presumably as far as the Harbour gates and by horses thereafter. 2-4-0T No. 118A was nevertheless 'on the Harbour' during the First World War and it may well have been based at Dingwall. 118A had moved to Wick by 1919 and later turned up on the Inverness Harbour branch, where it ceased working in 1921 - 1922.

LYBSTER

Opening in July 1903 the nominally independent Wick and Lybster Light Railway was worked by the Highland from the start and destined to be the final extension of their sphere of operation. A small wooden shed arranged in usual HR fashion was built beside the approach to the station and a 43ft 6inch turntable laid alongside. The rebuilt Jones 0-4-4T No. 53, which had started life on the Strathpeffer branch, worked the first train and became the regular engine until it was withdrawn in 1929, carrying the name *Lybster* for most of its life. A Drummond 0-4-4T also appeared on occasion and became the regular type after the departure of No. 53 (latterly 53A) until the line was closed, relieved at times by a small Caledonian 0-4-4T, No. 15103, and less often by a Yankee 4-4-0T, a class which appeared rather heavy for the line. Normally the spare engine was kept at Wick but the 1919 allocation shows two engines at Lybster, 0-4-4T No. 45 together with *Lybster*. Both of course would not have been at the shed at the same time; one would be working the branch, the other at Wick for whatever attention might be necessary.

Highly vulnerable to road transport on the parallel A9, the Light Railway was closed to all traffic 'temporarily' in April 1944, a closure made permanent in 1949. The station, goods shed etc. were still intact in 1955 but the shed had been reduced to its foundations.

MUIR OF ORD

An official plan shows a turntable at Muir of Ord and a building alongside with every appearance of an engine shed. This, however, is far from conclusive evidence; the branch engine was kept at Fortrose and any idea of a shed at Muir of Ord might be forgotten but for a typically cryptic Highland Minute of 1918, seeking authority for 'an Engine Shed at Muir of Ord'. There is no other indication whether it might be a replacement, or a wholly new shed and in any event the idea went no further.

PERTH

After Inverness, Perth was the principal engine shed of the line, but little is known of its early history. The first section of what was to become the Highland main line was that from Stanley Junction to Dunkeld, the 'Perth and Dunkeld Railway', opened in April 1856. There was an engine shed and turntable at Dunkeld, put in by the Perth and Dunkeld, but the line at this stage was worked by the Scottish North Eastern, with no need for a separate engine shed at Perth. This changed in 1863 when the line opened throughout, the 'Inverness and Perth Junction Railway' - the intervening 103 miles or so - coming into use amid great confusion. Insufficient

15051 outside Lybster shed in the mid 1930s. The line was effectively overcome by road traffic prior to 1939, but remained open to 1944 for 'strategic reasons'. *Photo:- W.A.Camwell*

The Highland shed at Perth, as the LMS 'Perth North' on 7th June 1936. The 'new standards' were very much in evidence, with 4-6-0s Nos. 5008, 5009, 5026, 5082, 5083, 5084, 5085, 5086, 5162, 5163, 5164, 5165 and 5166, Hughes Moguls 2805 and 2806, 4F 0-6-0s Nos. 4315 and 4317 and standard 3F tank No. 7329. Now this was an up to date complement, to stand comparison with any shed in the LMS and only four pre - Grouping types were in evidence. *Photo:- W.A.Camwell*

engines had been delivered for the work and some had to be borrowed. A small building formerly of the Scottish Midland Junction was handed over to the Inverness and Perth Junction on 1st May 1863 (a sale proper seems to have been completed in 1866/67) and became the engine shed; the building at Dunkeld went out of use around the same time and was subsequently dismantled, parts at least, to be utilised elsewhere.

The Perth shed was less than suited to the work and on 2nd November 1864 it was 'Resolved . . . . . . to accept the Tender of James Orr of £685 . . . . . . for the enlarging of the Engine Shed at Perth'. Whatever improvements Orr was able to effect the building was inadequate and was finally replaced by a stone built shed of eight roads, sited a little north of the General station on the down side. It was in two identical sections, and possessed of a handsome if archaic frontage of arches. Its appearance places its construction, in probability, in the 1870s, though no precise dates are known; it may very well date from rather later - a Perth newspaper for instance makes a report in 1886, suggesting that the Highland engine shed is to be 'reconstructed'. The shed was furthermore 'renewed in parts' during 1897 when presumably the old Scottish Midland Junction shed was still standing, for instructions were issued for 'the old shed . . . . .to be left for use of wagon or carriage repairs'.

A coaling bench was tucked away at the back of the shed on the west side, while the turntable was at the north end of the shed yard. At first 45 ft. in length, it was extended to 53 ft. 9 ins. by 1901 and later to 54 ft. 9 ins.

In Highland days most of the principal main line classes were allocated to Perth, together with an 0-6-0T for yard shunting and two or three 4-4-0Ts one employed at Aberfeldy and another as passenger pilot at the north end of Perth. In 1919 the 32 engines at Perth were:

Clan 4-6-0 : 49 *Clan Campbell* , 51 *Clan Fraser*, 52 *Clan Munro*
Castle 4-6-0 : 28 *Cluny Castle*, 29 *Dalcross Castle*, 35 *Urquhart Castle*, 50 *Brodic Castle*, 58 *Darnaway Castle*, 59 *Foulis Castle*, 147 *Beaufort Castle*, 149 *Duncraig Castle*
Superheated Goods 4-6-0 : 77, 78
Big Goods 4-6-0 : 103, 106, 107, 109
Small Ben 4-4-0 : 1 *Ben-y-Gloe*, 17 *Ben Alligan*
Loch 4-4-0 : 122 *Loch Moy*, 123 *Loch an Dorb*, 127 *Loch Garry*, 130 *Loch Fannich*
Barny 0-6-0 : 18, 19, 138, 139
Banking Tank 0-6-4T : 42, 44
0-6-0T : 24
4-4-0T : 58A, 59A

Perth on 13th June 1936. The mix of locomotives was very much the same as the previous week (see first view, page 119), an interesting combination given that plans were already afoot for the closure of the shed and its merger into a new, modern depot to be raised up on the site of the old Caledonian 'Friarton' shed. (see Volume 5 *The Caledonian Railway*, Wild Swan Publications).

Photo:- W.A.Camwell

After the grouping the Highland shed became known as Perth North but was very largely independent from the decaying Caledonian structure at Friarton until the latter's reconstruction in 1936 - 8 (See Volume 5).

When increased power became sorely needed for the Highland Main Line in the late 1920s the first step was the return of the six River Class 4-6-0s (see reference under Inverness) in 1928, Nos. 14756-61. In the following year ten new Hughes Moguls, Nos. 13100-9 arrived and earlier seven standard 4F 0-6-0s, Nos. 4312-8. All these were stationed at Perth North displacing most of the Highland engines which were moved north. Indeed by mid-1935 the Highland was represented at Perth by only four Castles, Nos. 14678/84/90/1, and the six Rivers. A Caledonian 0-4-4T was now supplied to Aberfeldy, a Standard 0-6-0T was the yard shunter and a Caledonian 0-4-4T the passenger pilot. By 1934 Blair Atholl had become part of the Perth District but maintained a fairly constant allocation of 4-4-0s and banking engines.

The Stanier Class 5s which arrived in Scotland in 1934 at first worked from Perth North to Inverness, Nos. 5021-9 were there by the end of September of that year, but some 26 were allocated to Inverness and to Perth South where there was ultimately an unrivalled concentration of the class.

The new depot at Friarton (Perth South) slowly took shape from 1936 but the Highland shed was still very much in business in July 1937 when on a Sunday visit the undernoted were seen:

Hughes	2-6-0 :		2806
Standard	4F	0-6-0 :	4315/7

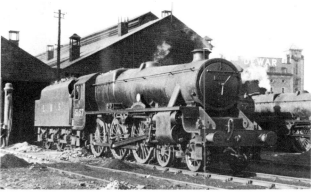

A 'new one', 4-6-0 No. 5157 *The Glasgow Highlander.*
Photo:- The Late George Ellis, cty, Bruce Ellis

A contrast from the previous views - Perth in July 1933 before the main influx of the 'new engines'
Photo:- D.E.White

17415 amidst snowploughs around 1930. *Photo:- Gordon Coltas*

Crab 2-6-0, one of the first standard types to begin the transformation of the work on the Highland, at Perth c.1930. They had a relatively brief stay, giving way to the more versatile class 5 4-6-0s and little records survives of the work performed by these engines, other than it was 'most capable'.
Photo:- Gordon Coltas

Hughes 2-6-0 : 2806
Standard 4F 0-6-0 : 4315/7
Class 5 4-6-0 : 5018/81/2/4/6/7, 5163/5/7/71, 5359
Standard 0-6-0T : 7329
H.R. Castle : 14678 (14691 was under repair at Perth South)

River 4-6-0 : 14756
C.R. 0-4-4T : 15144/71, 15218
C.R. 2F 0-6-0 : 17442
Once the new arrangements at Perth South were completed the final part of the project, the abandonment of Perth North, could take place and it is believed that final transfer of men and engines took place on 14th May 1938. This then can be regarded as the closure date of the shed but it did serve as a store for locomotives; twenty were laid up there in 1939 and were no doubt swiftly returned to service after the outbreak of war.

Subsequently the section of the Highland shed furthest from the main line was demolished but the other half, substantially unaltered, was retained as an engineer's store, a role in which it serves still. (May 1989)

Gordon Castle on **29th May 1930**
Photo:- T.Middlemass

4-6-0 No. 14680 *Murthly Castle* at Perth Shed. *Photo:- R.S.Carpenter*

Perth with its complement of Crab 2-6-0s in June 1937. 2800 - 2809 had arrived at the shed in 1928, to join the River 4-6-0s, HR engines sold new to the Caledonian in 1915 and reinstated to the line for which they were designed only in 1928. All were resident at Perth until 1935 but with Black 5s increasingly available withdrawals began the following year. *Photo:-Photomatic*

14392 *Loch Naver* at the north end of the yard around 1930. The Highland engines had largely gone by 1935, following the arrival the previous August / September of new Class 5s 5021 - 5029.

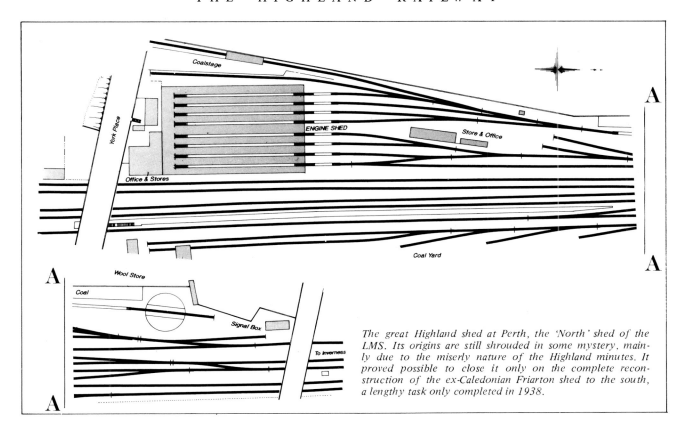

The great Highland shed at Perth, the 'North' shed of the LMS. Its origins are still shrouded in some mystery, mainly due to the miserly nature of the Highland minutes. It proved possible to close it only on the complete reconstruction of the ex-Caledonian Friarton shed to the south, a lengthy task only completed in 1938.

4-6-0 No. 58 *Darnaway Castle* **at Perth in 1923.** *Photo:- Authors Collection*

Portessie on 1st. May 1936, long years after closure as an engine shed. Mouldering quietly amid fields it long stood testimony to the commercial misjudgement which brought the Highland into the Buckie fish trade. *Photo:- E.W.Hannan*

The business fell away largely through natural causes; fish were increasingly disinclined to inhabit the seas round about and larger fishing boats were unsuited to the small harbour. Latterly traffic accounted to little more than erratic despatches of the Aultmore Distillery. *Photo;- E.W.Hannan*

Portessie on 9th June 1936. The shed saw some further humble use and a few pounds filtered back into the Highland coffers : *30th June 1914. Application to use Portessie Engine Shed and Grounds for making and storing concrete blocks. Recomend a rent of £25 p.a. .... Engineer to lay rails into shed ...... at a cost of £90 which will be charged to capital.* Photo:- E.W.Hannan

PORTESSIE

The straggling branch northwards from Keith to Portessie ended a mile from the Buckie station of the Great North of Scotland Railway; it was an attempt on the Buckie fish trade which, unfortunately, was already in in decline. Opened with the branch in 1884 the shed, suprisingly built in brick, had two roads, in anticipation of the goods traffic. In the event it was never necessary to house more than a single engine and the first occupant was a Jones 2-4-0 tank No. 59 *Highlander* altered in 1887 to a 4-4-0T. In 1889 it figured in a collision at Keith when leaving with the 3.40pm to Portessie, colliding with some empty coaches. By 1900 it had departed and in 1901 a Yankee Tank No. 54 was the branch engine and bore the name *Portessie*. In 1903 it was transferred to Fort Augustus and no firm information is available as to what took over. Most probably it was a member of the same class as the line was steeply graded and required a capable engine.

Portessie shed was closed in November 1907, the timetable altered to enable services to be operated from the Keith end. It remained in industrial use for a number of years but by the 1950s only the base of the water tank remained, although the site of the shed was clear.

The line, officially known as the Buckie Branch, was closed to all traffic in August 1915 and the rails were lifted to be used for military purposes. It was relaid after the war but services were never resumed other than at the south end where freight was operated (until 1966) to a distillery at Aultmore, 2½ miles from Keith. The 45ft. turntable at Portessie was still there in 1920.

SPEAN BRIDGE

In addition to the shed at Fort Augustus the Invergarry & Fort Augustus Railway provided a smaller single-road version of very similar construction at the other end of the line at Spean Bridge. It does not seem to have ever been used for its intended purpose but has long survived the closure of the branch, and is still in industrial use. Located at the Fort William end of the station on the up side of the main line, it is visible from passing West Highland trains.

The Highland took on not only one distantly seperate shed but two, moreover the second almost certainly was never used, which puts Spean Bridge into possibly the queerest category of 'LMS Engine Sheds' yet described.
Photo:- W.A.Camwell

The Highland worked the line from 1903 to 1907, when it gave up the branch to some relief. Certainly the shed yard seems to have been used in that time, for the turntable well long held engine ashes. The North British used the shed as a District Engineers store but later the various items of gear were removed to Fort William. The shed was decrepit, with buffer stops outside by 1939 but was late given over to private use, and stands today.   *Photo:- W.A.Camwell*

STROME FERRY

Strome Ferry was the terminus of the Dingwall & Skye line from 1870 until 1897, nearly thirty years. An elaborate pier had been developed with a two road shed 70ft. by 30ft. to serve the terminus; access was direct from a '43ft. 7inch' turntable, in the Highland tradition of peculiar dimensions*, and the building was in timber. The location was on the down side at the Inverness end of the station. It was 'only temporary' before the extension on to Kyle but eluded fire and tempest with greater facility than many of its contemporaries. Gradients are severe between Dingwall and Strome Ferry and the meagre service began at first with 5 ft. 2-4-0s. The rigid wheelbase was deleteriously affected by the curvatures found on the line and in 1871 Jones obtained permission from the Board to alter two of the 2-4-0s to 4-4-0s, using Adams bogies. Nos. 7 and 10 were afterwards considered a success, though they were assisted by 2-4-0s as occasion demanded. The pair formed the basis of the Skye Bogies and both doubtless spent time at Strome Ferry shed.

In an enchanting account of a journey north from Kyle (having travelled by steamer from Liverpool), T.R. Perkins (*The 'Farthest North' British Railway, The Railway Magazine*, August 1904) describes Strome Ferry: '. . . . . . . its glory now departed, and the engine shed which formerly stood near the station has been demolished, the pit over which the engines stood being still visible'.

* Dimensions appear to have been calculated strictly in relation to wheelbase - a Skye Bogie was 42ft. 9inches, so the Strome Ferry 'table was arranged to give a 5 inch clearance at each end. The opening to Kyle brought about the closure of Strome Ferry shed and it was quickly abandoned, it would seem, to fall into disrepair.

'The lane to the shore' at Strome Ferry, with the shed beyond, beneath the wooded slope. What remains of the Highland buildings today, and those of other railways in the north and west of Scotland, to Fort William and Oban, have a quaintness about them, a picturesque quality. When built however they were regarded almost with awe, for their great size and boldness of construction. To the villager emerging from under his turf roof the railway remained for years a thing of wonder. *Photo:- Gordon Coltas*

ACKNOWLEDGEMENTS

Strome Ferry at the turn of the century, the time of Perkins' visit to *the Farthest North..........its glory now departed.*
Photo:- J.L.Stevenson collection

LMS Engine Sheds began as a series a decade or more ago, to match at times the tortorous developments it has sought to chronicle. *Irwell Press* is the third publisher to have been associated with the books so long has been the road and so numerous and varied the contributions. It is difficult now to recall all the help so generously given and the many kindnesses (great and small) that have made it (mostly) a pleasure. The following must of necessity read like a list - Jones would have issued it as another fearsome *NOTICE* , to be read by order.

Thanks in especial are due to J. F. McEwan, as with most matters Scottish, to John and Christine, for all sorts of reasons, to Mavis and C. Brown, H. C. Casserley and R. M. Casserley and all the photographers mentioned throughout the book. Of the small band penetrating that misty far off region in the 1920s and 1930s H. C. Casserley and W. A. Camwell were prominent and between them have left a Highland annal without which coverage would be poor indeed. H. N. James was similarly intrepid and his expeditionary talents are devoted now to China and such places. In 1936 Scotland, relatively, was a more daunting prospect. Stephen Summerson 'made the trip' in the 1950s and his freely given time and insight has once again been of great value. Peter Tatlow's help, similarly, has been valued throughout.

With apologies for any omissions, we acknowledge with great thanks : Tom Middlemass, Brian Hilton, John Smith, Bernard Mathews, A. B. MacLeod, R. F. Roberts, Brian Morrison, W. T. Stubbs, Ken Fairey, R. D. Stephen, P. J. Kelley, P. J. Garland, E. W. Hannan, N. E. Preedy, Gordon Coltas, P. W. Melvill, Tony Wright, John Edgington, R.J. Buckley, The Committee of The Friends of the National Railway Museum, and the staff of the library there, A. E. Bennett, the late G. H. Platt, P. Hutchinson, A. R. Goult, D. E. White, the late A. G. Ellis and his son, Bruce Ellis, and in particular, BR staff at Buchanan House, Glasgow. A particularly valuable contribution, for its great age and careful preservation, has been made possible through the good offices of the University of Aberdeen. The George Washington Wilson collection preserved there represents a quite remarkable record of many aspects of life in Scotland so very long ago and deserves to be better known.

Two people who also deserve to be better known are Beverly and Wendy; they represent an unchanging and thereby all the more valued feature of this winding road of a series.

A feature of previous volumes (an attraction evidently, which is somewhat unsettling) has been an *errata/amendment* to previous volumes. Gratifyingly over the years it has steadily reduced in extent, apart from obvious typographical hiccups (*Balornock,* or even *Balornoch* and a mysterious 'J91'), so that it becomes possible to hide it away in the acknowledgements. The gremlins had a field day with the plan of Ladyburn - whilst fascinating for students of the might have been it owed little to reality; more to how the shed should have been rebuilt following the 'Blitz'. Only half the roof should have been shown of course, as depicted in the photographs on p75.

Students of the arcane, which must necessarily include engine sheds, could do worse than consult the journal of the Engine Shed Society, the aptly named *Link* , which exists to foster interest in the subject. Inquiries to : Paul Smith, Studio 726, Unit 210, Jubilee Trades Centre, Sherlock Street Birmingham B5 6ND.